CLOSING THE GAP

IN HOMEOWNERSHIP

Re-writing the Rules

Against Mortgage Discrimination

Anna DeSimone

HOUSING
RESEARCH
PRESS ——

First Edition: May 2024

Acknowledgement

Sources used in the preparation of this material include the following agencies and organizations. Citations are provided in the final pages of this book.

Appraisal Institute

Brookings Institute

Consumer Financial Protection Bureau

Core Logic

Environmental Protection Agency

Experian Credit

Fair Isaac Corporation

Fannie Mae

Federal Financial Institutions Examination Council

Federal Housing Finance Agency

Federal Reserve Board of Governors

Federal Reserve Bank of Minneapolis

Federal Reserve Bank of St. Louis

Foothold Technology

Freddie Mac

Joint Center for Housing Studies of Harvard University

Interagency Task for Property Appraisal Valuation Equity

International Energy Agency

National Association of Real Estate Brokers

National Association of Hispanic Real Estate Professionals

National Coalition for Community Reinvestment

National Council of State Housing Agencies

National Association of Realtors

Office of the Comptroller of the Currency

Oliver Wyman Company

The Policy Surveillance Program

TransUnion

U.S. Census Bureau

U.S. Centers for Disease Control

U.S. Department of Justice

U.S. Department of Housing and Urban Development

U.S. Department of Veterans Affairs

USDA Rural Housing Service

Contents

CHAPTER 1

Measuring the Gap

MORE THAN TEN MILLION PEOPLE BECAME HOMEOWNERS in the United States from 2012 to 2022. During this decade, people of color accounted for about 85% of household growth—and in 2022, 35% of all households were headed by a person of color.[1] In the year 2028, about 4.5 million Asian, Black, and Hispanic households will reach the median age for buying a home.[2]

Despite increasing diversity in America's population, homeownership rates for households of color continue to lag. In fact, the gap in homeownership between White and Black families is larger today than it was in 1960, before the passage of the Fair Housing Act of 1968.

TABLE 1 – NATIONAL RATE OF HOMEOWNERSHIP				
	WHITE	BLACK	HISPANIC	ASIAN*
Ownership Rate % →	73.8	45.9	49.8	63.0
GAP →		27.9	24.0	10.8

*Includes Native Hawaiian and Pacific Islander

Source: Federal Reserve Economic Data, 2023 Q4

Generations of racist housing practices have placed households of color at a disadvantage in terms of access to homeownership. Even in areas where households earn more than 120% of area median income, just 71% of Black households and 72% of Hispanic households own homes, compared with 85% of White households.[3]

The Wealth Gap

According to research completed by the Brookings Institute based on Federal Reserve data, between 2019 and 2022 median wealth increased by $51,800, but the racial wealth gap increased by $49,950. This adds up to a difference of $240,120 in wealth between the median White household and the median Black household.

"In 2022, for every $100 in wealth held by White households, Black households held only $15"

--Brookings Institute

Wealth measurement is based on the total value of assets a family owns (such as housing and business equity) minus their debts. Median Black wealth increased from $27,970 to $44,890, but continued to lag behind other racial groups, according to 2019-2022 Federal Reserve data. In 2022, median wealth was approximately $62,000 for Hispanic households.[4]

The Home Equity Gap

As of the fourth quarter of 2022, the average homeowner in America had $270,000 of equity in their home, after gaining $95,000 in the previous three years, according to *The State of the Nation's Housing Report 2023* from the Joint Center of Housing Studies (JCHS) of Harvard University, based on data from the Federal Reserve and Core Logic.[5]

When last measured by JCHS, the median home equity held by White homeowners was $130,000, nearly twice the amount of Black homeowners, at $68,800, and more than a third higher than that of Hispanic homeowners at $95,000.[6]

The Office of Economic Policy of the U.S. Department of the Treasury stated in its inequality blog series, *Racial Differences in Economic Security: Housing,* "In addition to the substantial sense of security that housing stability provides, homeownership imparts many economic benefits to households including unique access to leverage, a hedge against rising rents, tax deductions for mortgage interest and property taxes, low capital gains taxes relative to other investments, and, crucially, a vehicle for building wealth."[7]

Homeownership and Population Growth

U.S. Census reports indicate that from 2010 to 2020, White population has decreased by 8.6%.[8] Despite this decline, the rate of homeownership for White households increased from 74.4% in 2010 to 75% in 2020, according to the U.S. Department of Housing and Urban Development (HUD) National Housing Market Summary and Data.[9]

Population growth statistics from the Census Bureau report, *2020 Census Illuminates Racial Composition of the Country* [10] are highlighted below, along with key statistics from HUD homeownership data.[11]

- Hispanic and Latino population grew 23% between 2010 and 2020, while homeownership increased just 2.6%, from 47.5% to 50.1%.

- Asian population grew 35.5%, while homeownership increased by just 2%, varying between 57% and 59% throughout the decade.

- Black homeownership was 45.9% in 2010 and 45.9% in 2020 as well, with interim fluctuation ranging from 42% to 44%. During this time, Black population grew 4.5 million, or about 8%.

Foreign-born population in America reached 46.2 million people in 2022, or 13.9% of total population, according to the Census Bureau's *New Report on the Nation's Foreign-Born Population*. Almost half of all immigrants in the U.S. entered the country before 2000, and by 2028, the foreign-born share of population is projected to be higher than any time since 1850. [12]

Immigrants comprise more than one-fifth of the population in four states: California, Florida, New York and New Jersey. Foreign-born populations grew by 40% or more In Delaware, North Dakota, South Dakota and West Virginia. [13] The multiracial population represents people who identify as two or more races. The Census Bureau report, *2020 Census Illuminates Racial Composition of the Country,* stated:[14]

"America's multiracial population climbed from 9 million people in 2010 to 33.8 million people in 2020, showing an increase of 276%."

—U.S. Census Bureau

"Increasing numbers of recent immigrants are highly educated, and 47% have a bachelor's degree or higher, compared with 35% of native-born adults. Immigrants with more skills and education generally earn higher incomes and are better positioned to form new households, buy homes, and afford different areas than their counterparts with less income, illustrating a need for more diverse housing options."[15]

—Joint Center of Housing
Studies of Harvard University

Regulatory Action for Noncitizen Borrowers

In October 2023, the U.S. Department of Justice and the Consumer Financial Protection Bureau (CFPB) issued a *Joint Statement on Fair Lending and Credit Opportunities for Noncitizen Borrowers under the Equal Credit Opportunity Act*. The statement was issued as a reminder to financial institutions that credit applicants are protected from discrimination on the basis of their national origin, race, and other characteristics, even if they are not U.S. citizens or permanent residents. The Equal Credit Opportunity Act (ECOA) allows a creditor to consider immigration status when necessary to ascertain the creditor's rights regarding repayment.[16]

Cost Burdened Renters

The May 2023 Federal Reserve's *Report on the Economic Well-Being of U.S. Households in 2022* states that 27% of adults rent their homes in America, and that lower-income, Black, and Hispanic adults were disproportionately likely to rent as opposed to owning a home. Additionally, those who live in low- and moderate-income neighborhoods or who live in metro areas were more likely to be renters. Renters in 2022 were 22% White, 41% Black, 35% Hispanic, and 28% Asian.[17]

The Fed report also included results from the 2022 *Survey of Household Economics and Decision-making (SHED)*, where respondents indicated the reasons why they rent their homes. Many are renting instead of owning because of financial circumstances, and 32% of respondents stated they are trying to buy. The most cited reason for renting (65%) was an inability to afford a down payment, and 44% of respondents said they can't afford a monthly mortgage payment.[18]

An estimated 22.4 million Americans—about half of all renters—spend more than 30% of their monthly income on rent. Of those, 12 million renters pay 50% or more of their income toward rent.[19]

Households with housing expense greater than 30% of monthly income are considered cost burdened, and households with housing expense greater than 50% are considered severely cost burdened. Statistics from the Census Bureau's American Community Survey are highlighted below.[20]

- 57% of Black renter households are cost burdened and spend over 30% of their income on rent—and half of those households spend over 50% of their income on rent.

- 53% of Hispanic renters are cost burdened, including 28% who are severely cost-burdened.

- 44% of Asian renters are cost burdened, including 25% who are severely cost burdened.

- 49% of multi-race or other ethnic categories are cost burdened, including 27% are severely cost burdened.

Disparities in Home Affordability

For a consecutive 10-year period from 2011 to 2021, interest rates remained below 5% for 30-year fixed rate mortgages. In 2023, rising interest rates and home prices reduced home buying affordability for White renter households by 30%. The ability to afford a median-priced home in the U.S. dropped by 39% for Black renter households and dropped by 37% for Hispanic renter households.[21]

There are a number of states in the U.S. where opportunities for Black families to purchase a home have worsened, compared to other racial and ethnic groups. Nationally, there five states where only 5% of Black households can afford to buy a home in the state where they live, and about a dozen states where just 10% of Black households can afford a home in their state.[22]

How to Measure the Gap for any U.S. State

A homeownership gap is the difference between a geographical area's share of White households who own a home and another racial or ethnic group. As shown previously in Table 1, when the national homeownership rate for Blacks (45.9%) is subtracted from the figure for Whites (73.8%), the smaller number equates to a 27.9% gap. Two tables are included on the following pages, explained below.

Table 2 lists the 2023 rate of homeownership by race and ethnicity for each state, and a gap can be computed for any minority group. As an example, in Massachusetts, the White ownership rate is 69%. The Black/White gap is 31% [69 minus 38] and the Hispanic/White gap is 36% [69 minus 33].

TABLE 2 – HOMEOWNERSHIP BY STATE			
	White	Black	Asian	Hispanic
NATIONAL	73.8	45.9	63.0	49.8
Alabama	78	53	66	58
Alaska	71	38	64	51
Arizona	73	41	66	59
Arkansas	73	44	61	57
California	63	35	61	46
Colorado	70	42	65	57
Connecticut	74	44	63	42
Delaware	83	54	68	61
District of Columbia	47	34	39	44
Florida	75	48	72	55
Georgia	75	51	71	55
Hawaii	59	27	74	43
Idaho	74	30	66	60
Illinois	74	40	66	59
Indiana	76	39	60	58
Iowa	75	30	58	61
Kansas	71	39	63	58
Kentucky	73	39	60	46
Louisiana	78	49	73	56
Maine	75	27	64	54
Maryland	78	53	74	53
Massachusetts	69	38	58	33
Michigan	79	45	64	59
Minnesota	77	29	64	49
Mississippi	79	57	62	58
Missouri	72	41	55	56
Montana	71	29	55	54
Nebraska	70	32	55	51
Nevada	67	33	68	52
New Hampshire	74	36	65	39
New Jersey	76	40	66	42
New Mexico	73	48	63	71
New York	65	33	53	28
North Carolina	75	47	70	52
North Dakota	69	19	28	38
Ohio	73	38	61	52
Oklahoma	70	38	59	53
Oregon	66	27	64	44
Pennsylvania	74	45	62	48
Rhode Island	69	39	59	36
South Carolina	79	56	74	56
South Dakota	73	49	32	47
Tennessee	73	44	67	47
Texas	69	41	66	59
Utah	74	28	60	56
Vermont	75	30	53	65
Virginia	74	51	70	52
Washington	68	32	63	48
West Virginia	76	43	60	57
Wisconsin	73	26	56	47
Wyoming	74	19	40	65

Source: U.S. Census Bureau, Homeownership by State, 2023 4th Quarter

Table 3 denotes the change in homeownership rates from 2010 to 2020 for each U.S. state, ranked by the percent of change.

TABLE 3 – 10 YEAR CHANGE IN HOMEOWNERSHIP RATES			
U.S. State by Ranking	Difference	2010	2020
Hawaii	1.2	57.7	58.8
Alaska	0.8	63.1	63.9
Idaho	0.5	69.9	70.4
South Carolina	0.4	69.3	69.7
Wyoming	0.1	69.2	69.4
Maine	-0.2	71.3	71.1
New Hampshire	-0.5	71.0	70.5
Oregon	-0.5	62.2	61.7
Montana	-0.7	68.0	67.3
Arizona	-0.7	66.0	65.3
West Virginia	-0.8	73.4	72.6
Vermont	-0.8	70.7	69.9
New Mexico	-1.0	68.5	67.5
Colorado	-1.0	65.5	64.5
South Dakota	-1.1	68.1	67.0
Delaware	-1.2	72.1	70.8
Michigan	-1.2	72.1	70.9
Rhode Island	-1.3	60.7	59.4
California	-1.4	55.9	54.5
Utah	-1.4	70.4	69.0
Indiana	-1.5	69.9	68.4
Puerto Rico	-1.5	71.6	70.2
Mississippi	-1.5	69.6	68.2
Nebraska	-1.7	67.2	65.6
Washington	-1.7	63.9	62.2
Iowa	-1.7	72.1	70.4
Wisconsin	-1.7	68.1	66.3
Louisiana	-1.8	67.2	65.5
North Carolina	-1.8	66.7	64.9
Massachusetts	-1.9	62.3	60.4
Arkansas	-2.0	67.0	65.0
Alabama	-2.0	69.7	67.7
New York	-2.0	53.3	51.3
Nevada	-2.0	58.8	56.8
Ohio	-2.2	67.6	65.4
Kentucky	-2.2	68.7	66.4
Pennsylvania	-2.3	69.6	67.3
Florida	-2.3	67.4	65.1
Virginia	-2.4	67.2	64.9
Minnesota	-2.4	73.0	70.6
Kansas	-2.4	67.8	65.3
Maryland	-2.5	67.5	65.0
Texas	-2.5	63.7	61.2
Oklahoma	-2.6	67.2	64.7
Tennessee	-2.7	68.2	65.5
Georgia	-2.7	65.7	62.9
Missouri	-2.8	68.8	66.0
Illinois	-2.8	67.5	64.6
Connecticut	-3.3	67.5	64.2
District of Columbia	-3.7	42.0	38.3
North Dakota	-3.8	65.4	61.6
New Jersey	-4.2	65.4	61.3

Sources: U.S. Census Bureau, 2010 and 2020 Census Demographic and Housing Characteristics

CHAPTER 2

Lost Opportunities

EVERY YEAR THAT A PERSON OR HOUSEHOLD DOES NOT OWN A HOME they are losing the opportunity to build wealth and enhance their quality of life. Long delays—or being left out the home buying market altogether—can diminish a family's hope for long-term financial security. In addition to the financial benefits of homeownership, there is one type of lost opportunity that is immeasurable—the chance to raise a family in a healthy environment.

Healthier Homes

According to the U.S. Environmental Protection Agency (EPA), multifamily buildings have indoor air quality challenges since pollutants can move from unit to unit, and residents are unable to make changes or control the indoor air quality environment.[23] Exposure to secondhand smoke, mold, radon, and pest management are the leading health threats to the 80 million people in America who live in multi-unit buildings, according to the Centers for Disease Control and Prevention (CDC).[24]

Homeownership gives families a chance to mitigate the risk of exposure to environmental toxins and other harmful allergens. The International Energy Agency examined health outcomes in homes where ventilation and air quality improvements were completed, including improved heating systems, improved cooking systems, and air sealing. Healthier outcomes were listed as reduced symptoms of respiratory disease, asthma, cancer, cardiovascular disease, arthritis, and depression.[25]

Financial Incentives for a Sustainable Home

The United States Inflation Reduction Act of 2022 offers homeowners a chance to receive bottom-line tax credits of up to 30% on expenditures for home energy-efficiency improvements such as gas or electric heat pumps, air conditioning, insulation, hot water heaters, doors and windows, electrical panels, insulation, air sealing, and standalone generators.[26]

Mortgages are available that offer flexible qualifying rules for property renovations. Energy improvements can be financed 15% over the cost of a home purchase with a Fannie Mae *Home Style Energy®* or a Freddie Mac *Green Choice®* mortgage.[27] Loan qualification is expanded due to projected savings in utilities and maintenance for most conventional loan programs, as well as loans insured by FHA, VA, and USDA Rural Housing Service.

According to the NC Clean Energy Technology Center, there are more than two thousand state and federal financial incentives available to homeowners for energy improvements.[28] Financing is available to homeowners to help pay for energy audits, water testing and safety, mitigation of radon, mold, gas, and carbon monoxide, safe removal of asbestos and lead paint, weatherization, accessibility features, and steps to make the home climate resilient. Other incentives are often available to homeowners from their city or town housing authority or municipal agency.

Assistance with Weather Disasters

According to *The State of the Nation's Housing 2023* report by Harvard University's Joint Center for Housing Studies, 59.9 million households in America live in areas with at least a moderate threat from natural disasters.[29]

Fannie Mae's disaster response program offers homeowners assistance through Project Porchlight. Affected households receive a needs assessment and personalized recovery plan from trained disaster recovery experts and counselors approved by the U.S. Housing and Urban Development (HUD). Counselors provide ongoing guidance, check-ins, multiple language services, help with mortgage payment deferrals, and assistance with FEMA (Federal Emergency Management Agency) insurance claims or denials.[30]

Growth in Home Values

The most substantial lost opportunity is the chance to build a financial nest egg. Equity represents the current market value of a home minus any outstanding mortgages. Growth in home values varies by geographic region and can change based on a number of economic factors. As of September 2023, Americans were sitting on nearly $30 trillion in home equity, according to the St. Louis Federal Reserve Bank.[31]

The Federal Housing Finance Agency's House Price Index (FHFA HPI®) measures changes in single-family house values in 50 states and 400 cities. The FHFA HPI® projects what a house purchased at a given point in time would be worth today if it appreciated at the average appreciation rate of all homes in the area.[32]

Homes worth $300,000 in South Carolina increased in value by $147,000 in 36 months.

Purchase Quarter	Valuation Quarter	Table 4
2020 Quarter 4	2023 Quarter 4	Percentage Change
Purchase Value	Estimated Value for State	49.0%
$300,000	$447,000	

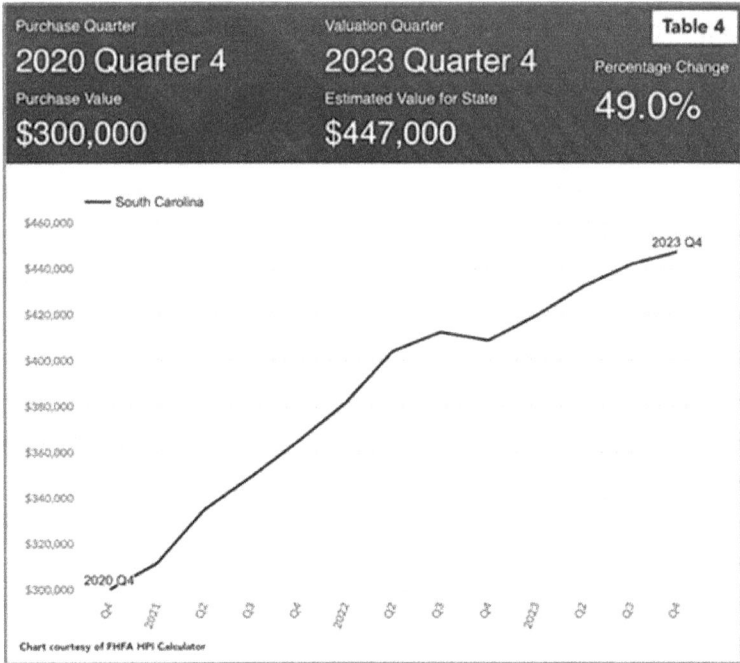

Chart courtesy of FHFA HPI Calculator

Table 4 reflects a 49.0% increase in value on a house purchased for $300,000 in the fourth quarter of 2020. The estimated value in the fourth quarter of 2023 for the home is $447,000.[33] This chart was produced using the FHFA HPI® Calculator, which estimates housing appreciation for all U.S. states and Metropolitan Statistical Areas (MSAs) for quarterly time periods as early as 1990. The tool can be accessed at www.fhfa.gov/datatools/tools/

According to the FHFA's February 2024 House Price Index Quarterly Report, the U.S. housing market has seen positive appreciation each quarter since the start of 2012. House prices rose 6.5% between the fourth quarter of 2022 and the fourth quarter of 2023, as shown in Table 5.[34]

U.S. House Price Appreciation
Purchase-Only FHFA HPI Over Previous Four Quarters

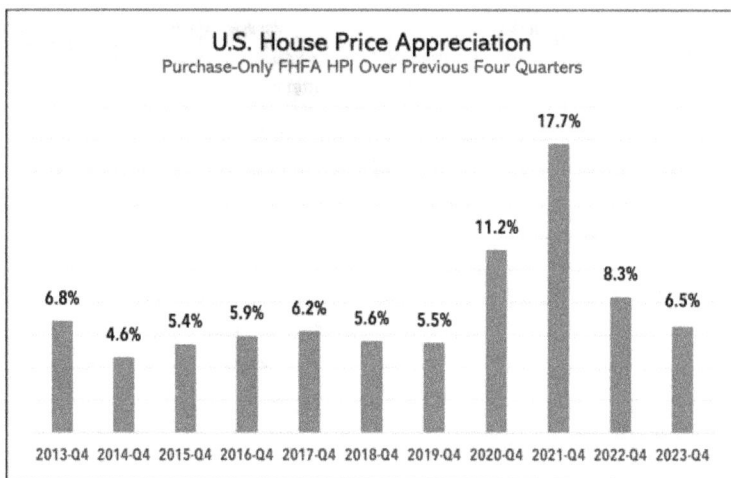

2013-Q4	2014-Q4	2015-Q4	2016-Q4	2017-Q4	2018-Q4	2019-Q4	2020-Q4	2021-Q4	2022-Q4	2023-Q4
6.8%	4.6%	5.4%	5.9%	6.2%	5.6%	5.5%	11.2%	17.7%	8.3%	6.5%

TABLE 5 - Source: Federal Housing Finance Agency, House Price Index (HPI) Quarterly Report

In the year 2021, house price appreciation accelerated to 17.7% as a result of the pandemic. This was triggered by a number of economic factors, including a shortage of new construction homes, supply chain constraints, work-at-home employment, and the need for socially-distanced housing.[35]

The FHFA HPI® Top 100 Metro Area Rankings measures changes in single-family house prices for the nation's top metro areas, which include major MSAs and Metropolitan Statistical Area Divisions (MSADs). As of the fourth quarter 2023, there were 20 metro areas with year-over-year (YoY) appreciation rates 10.0% and above, with the highest reaching 13.8% in the Miami-Miami Beach-Kendall, Florida metro. Of the 100 metros, 69 areas had YoY appreciation of 5.0% or more.

The FHFA HPI® Four Quarter Appreciation Map is another tool available to the public. Users can hover over any U.S. state to view appreciation rates, and MSA data is available for most states. Both the map tool and top metro rankings can be accessed at www.fhfa.gov/datatools/tools/

TABLE 6 – 2023 APPRECIATION RATE BY STATE

FHFA HPI Purchase-Only Four-Quarter House Price Change

State	Rate	State	Rate
Alabama	4.4	Montana	3.8
Alaska	5.7	Nebraska	4.9
Arizona	6.6	Nevada	3.4
Arkansas	5.9	New Hampshire	9.2
California	4.9	New Jersey	11.4
Colorado	3.3	New Mexico	5.1
Connecticut	12.9	New York	9.6
Delaware	4.7	North Carolina	7.0
District of Columbia	-1.2	North Dakota	4.9
Florida	6.8	Ohio	9.2
Georgia	7.2	Oklahoma	5.1
Hawaii	-3.4	Oregon	1.6
Idaho	0.5	Pennsylvania	6.9
Illinois	8.4	Rhode Island	15.1
Indiana	8.0	South Carolina	9.4
Iowa	5.6	South Dakota	6.8
Kansas	8.8	Tennessee	6.2
Kentucky	6.4	Texas	2.7
Louisiana	2.1	Utah	2.0
Maine	7.4	Vermont	13.3
Maryland	5.9	Virginia	7.3
Massachusetts	9.1	Washington	3.2
Michigan	9.7	West Virginia	12.4
Minnesota	4.1	Wisconsin	9.3
Mississippi	9.7	Wyoming	3.7
Missouri	8.0		

Source: Federal Housing Finance Agency Quarterly HPI Report

Table 6 shows the four-quarter appreciation rate by state, based on FHFA 2023 4Q data.

The Building Black Wealth Tour

Founded in 1947 by African American real estate professionals, the National Association of Real Estate Brokers (NAREB) launched a 100-city *Building Black Wealth Tour* in April 2024. The two-year tour will host events nationwide, offering festive activities for youths, and workshops on homeownership, property investment, starting a business, and other wealth-building opportunities. An internet feed will make virtual sessions and online conversations accessible to a national audience.[36] Detailed information and a list of tour stops are posted on the website www.narebblackwealthtour.com

NAREB advocates for equality in the real estate sector and formed a transformative partnership with the U.S. Department of Housing and Urban Development (HUD) in August 2023. According to HUD, "The collaboration is set to make significant strides in addressing appraisal bias and discrimination within the housing market, signaling advancement in housing equality."[37] HUD is also participating in NAREB's national *Building Black Wealth Tour.*

NAREB's annual report, *State of Housing in Black America (SHIBA)* outlines NAREB's policy priorities and recommendations to address barriers faced by Black homebuyers. A primary finding of NAREB's 2023 SHIBA Report is the importance of increased housing inventory to bolster Black homeownership. Other key findings include barriers related to credit scoring, disparate home appraisal practices, historical harm caused by environmental hazards in Black communities, and investors participating in the single-family housing market.[38] The 2023 SHIBA report can be accessed on www.nareb.com.

"There are more than two million mortgage-ready Black Americans. These families and individuals have the credit and income to qualify for a home mortgage."

—2023 State of Housing in Black America (SHIBA) Report

The Hispanic Wealth Project

The *Hispanic Wealth Project* (HWP) was established by the National Association of Hispanic Real Estate Professionals (NAHREP) in 2014. The Project orchestrates various initiatives to help the Hispanic community build wealth in three categories: homeownership, business ownership, and savings and investments. These initiatives include *NAHREP 10 Certified Trainers*, the HWP's *Angel Community*, and the *NAHREP REACH Labs*.

The Project is also committed to education, hosting various events and media, including the *Women Building Wealth* series, *Wealth Stream News*, and the annual *HWP Wealth Symposium*. Collectively, these programs and events further the HWP's goal to increase Hispanic household wealth, through increasing homeownership, scaling small businesses, and diversifying investments.[39]

The website is www.hispanicwealthproject.org

The *2023 State of Hispanic Homeownership Report* is a product of the National Association of Hispanic Real Estate Professionals and the *Hispanic Wealth Project*. The report combines research and data both within and outside of the housing industry. The report evaluates how the U.S. Latino population is faring in terms of homeownership acquisition and reviews the opportunities and barriers to future homeownership growth. Featured below are a few highlights from the report.[40]

- The growth of Hispanic homeownership has risen steadily for nearly a decade, and over 9.5 million Hispanic households now own their own home.

- Over the last ten years, Hispanic households have been responsible for 25.6% of the country's overall homeownership growth, despite only making up 14.8% of households.

- Latinos are the youngest racial or ethnic demographic in the U.S. purchasing homes, with a median age of 30.7, compared to the non-Hispanics with a median age of 41.1, more than 10 years older.

- Latinos continue to be among the most likely to live in multigenerational households, and comprised 31.4% of the market in 2022, compared to 18.0% of non-Hispanic households.

CHAPTER 3

Mortgage Denials

NEARLY SIX MILLION LOAN APPLICATIONS DID NOT CLOSE in 2022—more than 40% of all borrowers who applied for a mortgage.[41] Application fallout represents three possible outcomes: loans which are denied, applications withdrawn by the borrower, and files closed for incompleteness by the lender.

Table 7 reflects loan transactions from 4,460 banks, credit unions, and mortgage lenders.

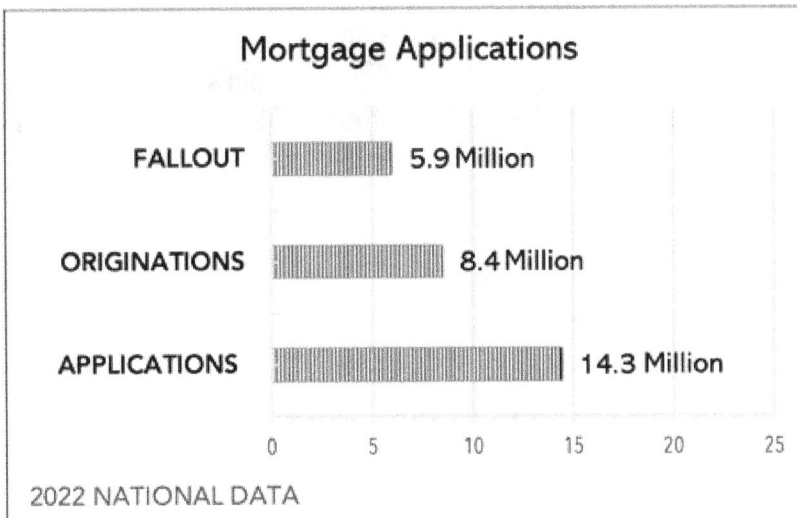

Mortgage Applications

Category	Value
FALLOUT	5.9 Million
ORIGINATIONS	8.4 Million
APPLICATIONS	14.3 Million

2022 NATIONAL DATA

TABLE 7 - Source: CFPB, 2022 HMDA Data Points Report

When mortgage applications are denied, borrowers are given a written explanation. People understand probabilities, and that loan approval cannot be guaranteed. However, there is little explanation as to why borrowers withdraw their application or why they give up on completing the process. Despite the probabilities, people begin their mortgage application with at least one expectation—their mortgage lender will stand behind a promise of good customer service.

Why Mortgage Applicants Walk Away

People put their trust in their loan originator, and they will cancel an application when that trust is lost. Borrowers need assurance that they are being presented with the full facts before paperwork is submitted. They need to know exactly what documents are required to verify funds and income—and they need to find out before they spend money on a home purchase deposit or pay for an appraisal or home inspection.

Borrowers sometimes feel that their loan application might be treated with less priority because their income is low, or where the home is located. Others may sense bias because of their race, ethnicity, gender, citizenship, domestic household structure, or handicap status. Households with limited English proficiency might question why foreign-language forms were not made available.

Table 8 denotes loan activity on applications submitted by Black borrowers in the Newark, New Jersey area in 2021, when interest rates were below 3%. Figures are segmented by applicant income, measured against census tract median income of the property location.[42]

BORROWER FALLOUT BY INCOME LEVEL Black Applicants - Newark, New Jersey MSA						
Tract Income	APPLICATIONS	ORIGINATED	DENIED	WITHDRAWN	INCOMPLETE	FALLOUT
Less than 50%	1,662	526	585	332	146	68%
50 - 79%	3,794	1,852	850	711	269	51%
80 - 99%	1,428	739	251	307	87	48%
100 - 119%	2,997	1,590	543	574	204	47%
120% & above	3,585	1,985	597	645	253	45%
Total Loans	13,046	6,692	2,826	2,569	959	49%

TABLE 8 - Source: CFPB 2021 HMDA Data, Newark MSA/MD (Newark NJ-PA)

For context, the median income in 2021 in the Newark NJ MSA was $86,445, and median property value was $483,500. Median age in the area is 39, and about 45% of the population have some college education.[43] In this analysis, 6,582 higher-income applicants applied for a mortgage, 1,140 were denied, and 1,676 walked away. The following year, interest rates doubled, and housing costs increased by 11.4%.

Denial Rates of Similarly Situated Borrowers

Three primary factors are used to determine mortgage eligibility—credit score, debt-to-income (DTI) ratio, and the combined loan-to-value (CLTV). Applicants whose loan characteristics are closely matched to other applicants are known as similarly situated borrowers. Although other factors are applied in fair lending analyses, disparate treatment can be uncovered on a broader scale based on the three primary factors (credit, debt, and CLTV).

Table 9 denotes key characteristics of 373,624 loan applications taken by nationwide lenders in the third quarter of 2023. The median values of all qualifying factors were marginally close, as noted below.

LOAN TRANSACTION CHARACTERISTICS				
	ASIAN	BLACK	HISPANIC	WHITE
Credit Score	768	735	748	763
CLTV	80.00	85.00	85.00	80.00
DTI Ratio	40.85	41.37	42.66	38.84
Interest Rate	6.625	6.750	6.875	6.875
Denial Rate	12.86	30.14	22.08	12.42

TABLE 9 - Source: CFPB Quarterly Graphs 2023-Q3, Conventional Conforming Loans

- **Across all groups, credit scores were within a 33-point range**

- **Across all groups, DTI ratios were within a 3.82% range**

Figures reflect originated and non-originated loan applications for conventional conforming purchase and refinance transactions. Loan activity was reported by a group of lenders known as Quarterly Filers, who collectively originate about half of the nation's mortgage volume each year.

In the analysis, Black and Hispanic applicants showed strong credit and affordability characteristics, yet their denial rates were significantly higher. Although there are other factors considered in loan approval, denial rates for Blacks and Hispanics in this example are not in alignment with Asian and White applicants with similar transaction characteristics.

Combined loan-to-value (CLTV) is derived by dividing the loan amount by the property value. For example, a mortgage of $240,000 on a $300,000 home equates to 80% CLTV. When there is a subordinate lien, the amounts are combined, and the sum is measured against property value.

The DTI ratio compares the combined gross monthly income of all applicants against total monthly debts. Debts include the total housing payment, known as PITI (principal, interest, taxes, and insurance) plus any monthly premiums for FHA or private mortgage insurance (PMI). Even though condo dues are not included in payments made to the lender, the monthly cost is factored into qualifying ratios.

Monthly debt payments include fixed payment amounts with 10 or more remaining payments, such as a car loan or child support. Based on current balances on revolving credit cards, lenders will project a monthly payment based on 5% of the total amount owed. As an example, a monthly PITI of $1,500, plus $350 for an auto loan, plus $150 for credit cards [$3,000 x .05%] adds up to $2,000. When $2,000 is divided by $6,000 gross monthly income, the DTI ratio is .33%.

Home Mortgage Disclosure Act

The Home Mortgage Disclosure Act (HMDA) was enacted by Congress in 1975, and rule-writing authority was transferred to the Consumer Financial Protection Bureau (CFPB) in 2011. The regulation helps determine whether financial institutions are meeting the credit needs of their communities, and also identify possible discriminatory lending patterns. Banks, credit unions, and mortgage companies meeting certain asset size or loan volume must submit a Loan Application Register (LAR) to the Federal Financial Institutions Examination Council (FFIEC) on an annual basis.

Each institution transmits over 100 elements of statistical data for every loan application it receives, including loans that were denied, withdrawn, closed for incompleteness, and pre-approval requests. A partial list of data collected include race, ethnicity, and other demographics for each person listed on the loan application, the property location census tract, loan type, interest rate, points, property type, loan purpose, occupancy, CLTV, action taken by the lender, and reason(s) for denial.

HMDA reports do not contain borrower names, street addresses, or any identifying information. Reports are made public the following year data collection, and additional confidential data is redacted. High-volume lenders must file reports on quarterly basis, and key statistics are released in advance by the CFPB based on quarterly filers data.[44] Anyone can research HMDA data at www.consumerfinance.gov

Denial Rates by Loan Type

The rate of denial for mortgages vary, depending upon the loan program and loan purpose. Historically, denial rates are higher for refinance transactions and mortgages insured by the Federal Housing Administration (FHA). Loans which are not insured by a government agency such as FHA, VA, or Rural Housing, are called conventional conforming loans and maximum loan limits are set annually by the Federal Housing Finance Agency.

Table 10 reflects nationwide home purchases for FHA and conventional conforming loans.

Rate of Mortgage Denial
ALL HOME PURCHASES

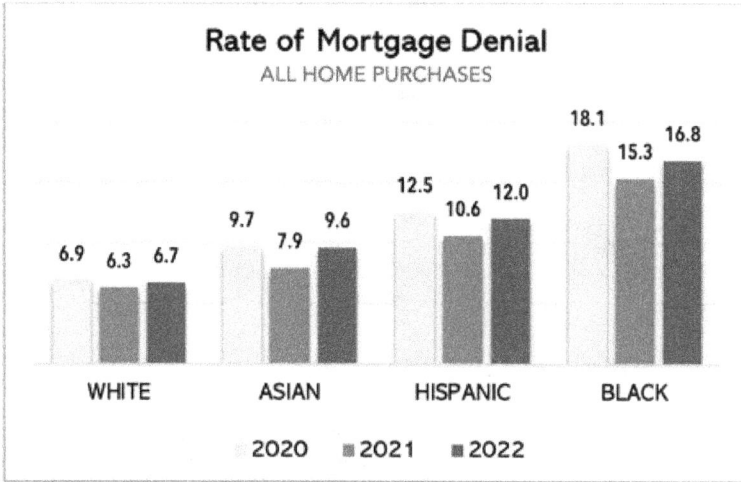

	WHITE	ASIAN	HISPANIC	BLACK
2020	6.9	9.7	12.5	18.1
2021	6.3	7.9	10.6	15.3
2022	6.7	9.6	12.0	16.8

TABLE 10 – CFPB HMDA Data Point Annual Reports 2020 - 2022.

Denial rates for purchase transactions shown in Table 10 are relatively consistent within each racial or ethnic group, despite interest rate changes over the 3-year period. For refinances, overall denial rates for all applicants in 2022 were 20.2% for Whites, 22.9% for Asians, 27.6% for Hispanics, and 35.8% for Blacks. For FHA loans, denial rates for both purchases and refinances in 2022 were 36.7% for Whites, 43.8% for Asians, 38.0% for Hispanics, and 45.0% for Blacks.[45]

Mortgage denial rates by race and ethnicity for each U.S. state in Table 11.

TABLE 11 – MORTGAGE DENIAL RATES				
	White	Black	Asian	Hispanic
Alabama	16.75	29.47	13.77	22.65
Alaska	10.93	18.18	15.85	14.89
Arizona	14.98	21.25	13.80	19.49
Arkansas	16.97	32.43	12.04	21.53
California	15.86	21.94	15.70	20.22
Colorado	13.15	20.19	13.98	20.63
Connecticut	15.56	24.25	15.77	21.88
Delaware	15.48	15.07	14.32	23.61
District of Columbia	9.55	24.81	12.42	18.35
Florida	19.22	26.91	18.67	24.32
Georgia	16.04	25.14	13.60	21.52
Hawaii	17.85	18.93	20.07	23.80
Idaho	12.95	17.38	13.08	18.77
Illinois	14.29	25.13	13.75	20.48
Indiana	14.36	23.65	13.27	19.70
Iowa	10.56	17.92	10.54	15.39
Kansas	13.75	23.68	15.42	19.98
Kentucky	17.45	22.36	13.43	21.21
Louisiana	17.04	32.67	15.43	23.08
Maine	14.56	17.80	15.31	20.01
Maryland	14.80	22.72	16.97	21.69
Massachusetts	14.20	25.86	14.21	23.17
Michigan	15.61	28.38	14.90	24.15
Minnesota	11.45	20.25	14.18	19.26
Mississippi	18.20	35.55	16.58	26.56
Missouri	13.44	24.16	12.81	20.44
Montana	13.55	22.30	16.78	21.68
Nebraska	10.97	21.22	10.55	17.70
Nevada	16.27	22.30	18.28	20.96
New Hampshire	16.09	23.65	17.05	23.14
New Jersey	16.48	24.88	15.70	22.69
New Mexico	16.53	21.01	16.43	22.01
New York	16.55	27.57	16.47	25.27
North Carolina	14.38	24.57	11.74	20.68
North Dakota	9.64	12.35	16.15	18.46
Ohio	16.00	26.06	14.28	22.00
Oklahoma	16.33	24.97	14.93	20.90
Oregon	13.86	19.81	14.55	19.87
Pennsylvania	16.49	29.07	15.35	24.42
Rhode Island	16.50	25.21	18.23	26.60
South Carolina	15.15	30.57	14.27	22.96
South Dakota	9.64	18.16	10.23	16.89
Tennessee	14.97	26.04	15.25	21.14
Texas	17.17	23.66	12.24	23.54
Utah	13.31	22.61	13.61	20.76
Vermont	13.89	20.21	16.29	17.66
Virginia	14.10	22.68	15.93	19.78
Washington	14.31	21.77	15.82	20.94
West Virginia	19.89	23.03	15.29	21.84
Wisconsin	11.56	25.55	12.86	19.98
Wyoming	13.58	16.30	15.95	19.20

Source: CFPB, 2022 HMDA

Reasons for Denial

According to the CFPB, Black and Hispanic borrowers were denied loans at higher rates, received smaller loans, were charged higher interest rates, and paid more in upfront fees than White and Asian borrowers in 2022. Lenders increasingly denied applicants for insufficient income, and loan applications were denied because of insufficient income at higher rates than at any point since that data was first collected and reported in 2018, according to the CFPB report.[46]

A study completed by the Federal Reserve Bank of Minneapolis examined differences in denial rates by race and ethnicity for conventional mortgage applications for home purchases for loan applications taken from 2018 to 2020. Federal Reserve Banks have access to confidential HMDA data and were able to incorporate additional loan characteristics in the study.

Results of the study were published in the January 2024 report, *Lender-reported reasons for mortgage denials don't explain racial disparities*, which stated, "Black applicants are 2.9 percentage points more likely to have their mortgage application denied relative to White applicants, while Asian and Latinx applicants are 2.2 percentage points and 1.5 percentage points respectively more likely to be denied."[47]

"An applicant of color is more likely to have their application denied than a White applicant with the same income and credit score who applies for a conventional mortgage of the same size for a similar home."

—Federal Reserve Bank of Minneapolis

The far-reaching study covered 6.1 million mortgage applications based on confidential HMDA datasets along with others' analysis of the same data. The study evidenced that independent mortgage companies and lenders that sell a high proportion of their loans have the lowest denial rates and smallest racial disparities in denial rates. After completing the analysis, Fed analysts interviewed mortgage lenders and underwriters for their perspectives on the findings. Interviewees pointed out that "mortgage officers might not provide the level of service that applicants of color sometimes need, resulting in more denials for procedural reasons."[48]

Table 12 denotes the reason for denial based on the analysis by the Federal Reserve Bank of Minneapolis. The report stated that HMDA data challenge the common narratives about denial reasons, and that reasons cannot be fully accounted for when examining other data.[49]

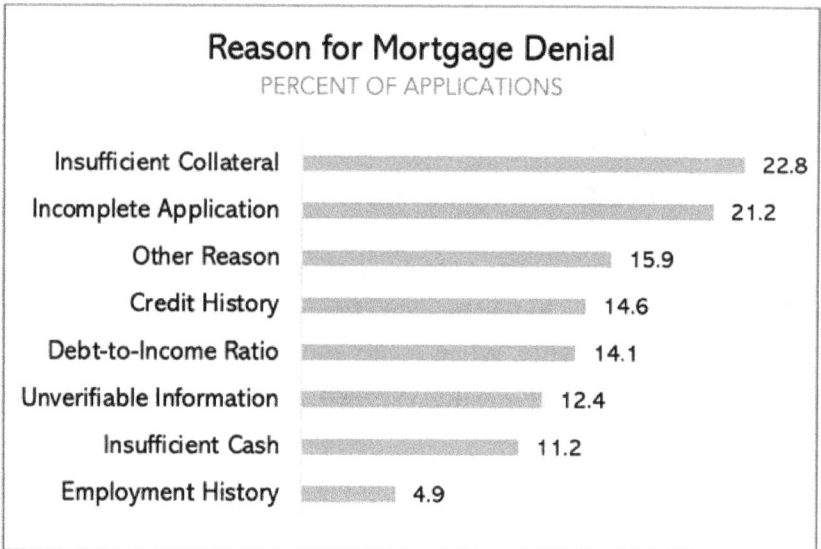

Reason for Mortgage Denial
PERCENT OF APPLICATIONS

Reason	Percent
Insufficient Collateral	22.8
Incomplete Application	21.2
Other Reason	15.9
Credit History	14.6
Debt-to-Income Ratio	14.1
Unverifiable Information	12.4
Insufficient Cash	11.2
Employment History	4.9

TABLE 12 - Source: Federal Reserve Bank of Minneapolis

Lenders can report up to 4 reasons for denial from a list of 8. Statistical analyses of HMDA data generally tabulate the *highest count* of a parameter. As stated in its report, what the Federal Reserve Bank study determined was the *most important reason.*

- <u>Insufficient collateral</u> is the number one reason for denial, due to appraisal valuations that are lower than the purchase price.

- <u>Incomplete application</u> is the second most common reason and may be attributed to the lender's quality of assistance.

- <u>Unverifiable information</u> underscores the necessity for lenders to provide clear instructions about verification steps.

Adverse Action Notification Rules

The Equal Credit Opportunity Act (ECOA) is a civil rights law enacted in 1974. ECOA makes it unlawful for any creditor to discriminate against any applicant on the basis of race, color, religion, national origin, sex (including sexual orientation and gender identity), marital status, and age, as long as the applicant is old enough to enter into a contract. The law protects applicants whose income is derived from any public assistance program (such as Social Security), or if the applicant has in good faith exercised their rights under certain consumer protection laws.[50]

ECOA requires mortgage lenders to issue a notice of adverse action when an application is denied within 30 days of receipt of a completed application.

The regulation requires lenders to provide a statement of specific reasons for the action taken in the adverse action notice. Specific reasons must relate to—and accurately describe—the factors considered or scored by a creditor.

Applicants have up to 60 days to request more information explaining the circumstances for the denial. By law, lenders must provide the name, address, and telephone number of the person or office from which the statement of reasons can be obtained. Applicants can request a written statement following an explanation given in person or by telephone.[51]

The Fair Credit Reporting Act (FCRA) requires lenders to provide a credit score notice to each person on the application, indicating the score used in making the credit decision.[52]

Artificial Intelligence in Credit Denials

September 19, 2023, the Consumer Financial Protection Bureau issued a mandate requiring creditors to incorporate additional specificity in adverse actions based on artificial intelligence (AI) or complex credit models. Credit decisions based on certain types of algorithms, known as uninterpretable or "black-box" models, make it difficult—if not impossible—to identify specific reasons of denial. According to the mandate, ECOA rules for adverse action apply equally to all credit decisions, regardless of the technology used to make them. Lending decisions based on AI must be "explainable" artificial intelligence, also known as XAI.[53]

A report by the Brookings Institute, *An AI Fair Lending Policy Agenda*, states "Artificial intelligence and machine learning models offer benefits, but they also have the potential to perpetuate, amplify, and accelerate historical patterns of discrimination. Because models are trained on historical data that reflect and detect existing discriminatory patterns or biases, their outputs will reflect and perpetuate those same problems. Algorithmic systems often have disproportionately negative effects on people and communities of color."[54]

Kristen Clarke, Assistant Attorney General for Civil Rights, U.S. Department of Justice, delivered the remarks featured below at the March 2024 America's Credit Union's Governmental Affairs Conference.[55]

"Financial institutions are collecting and using large amounts of consumer data to make predictions and decisions in the context of underwriting, pricing, and loan requirements, as well as advertising for all types of loans—including home loans. Purportedly neutral algorithms can end up amplifying or reproducing unlawful biases that have long existed around race, homeownership, and access to credit in the United States."

Automated Underwriting Systems

Just about every mortgage lender in America utilizes a technology known as an automated underwriting system (AUS), particularly for loans backed by government agencies. Fannie Mae's system is the Desktop Underwriter (DU), Freddie Mac's system is the Loan Product Advisor (LPA), and FHA's credit risk scorecard is called TOTAL. AUS systems incorporate algorithms to determine a "race-blind" risk rating of a mortgage application. Lenders have the option to underwrite loans manually to confirm fair and impartial standards.

The *2023 State of Housing in Black America (SHIBA)* report by the National Association of Real Estate Brokers stated "The AUS loan outcomes for purchase applications taken in 2022 were as follows: 70% of loan applications from Blacks evaluated with AUS were approved, of which 67% resulted in loan origination. In contrast, 80% of loan applications from Whites that were evaluated with AUS were approved, of which 78% resulted in loan origination."[56]

New Credit Scoring Models

The Federal Housing Finance Agency has led a multi-year effort to modernize credit scoring models to help improve accuracy in credit reporting, provide more inclusive credit scores, and expand equitable access to credit. In addition to the new scoring models, FHFA approved the use of two reports from national credit reporting agencies—instead of three—for underwriting mortgages. Fannie Mae and Freddie Mac have enhanced their automated underwriting systems with the new scoring criteria.

A credit score is a numerical value derived from a modeling system used to predict the likelihood of borrower default and establish the level of risk to the lender. The new scoring models are called FICO 10T and Vantage Score 4.0, described below.

- Alternative credit data – Vantage Score 4.0 takes into account payment histories for rent, utilities, telecom, etc. which can help applicants with limited credit experience generate a score.

- Trended data – FICO 10T and Vantage Score 4.0 evaluate the past 24 months of credit history, whereas the Classic FICO evaluated credit on the day the report was ordered.

What to do When a Mortgage Application is Denied

Applicants who are denied due to incomplete information are often able to re-submit their application with new appraisal information or other documents that boost loan qualification. People apply for loans in good faith and believe that the documents necessary to support their loan application will be attainable. However, there can be obstacles beyond their control.

Sometimes an applicant's employer will not respond to a lender's request to confirm employment, or answer questions regarding work hours or overtime pay. Sometimes a landlord refuses to complete a request form verifying rental payment history. These types of situations can be emotional and add to the stress of buying a home. Meeting with a certified homebuyer counselor can make a difference in dealing with a loan denial, appraisal issue, help with re-applying, or buying a new home. *(See Chapter 8, Find an Advocate.)*

If a loan is denied based on credit history, a good first step is to obtain a copy of the credit report to make certain all information is correct. The nation's three major credit agencies, (Equifax, Experian, and TransUnion) offer tools for consumers to mitigate errors. From the main website of any agency, instructions are provided on how to obtain a free credit report, file a dispute with a creditor, add a statement of explanation for a delinquent item, or take steps to boost a credit score.

Denials that are based on a lower appraisal valuation typically require homebuyers to increase their down payment. Steps for dealing with undervalued appraisals are explained in Chapter 5, Appraisal Bias.

The Market Insights Team at Freddie Mac conducted a study in April 2022 among consumers whose mortgage application had been denied in the past four years. The survey oversampled for Black and Hispanic consumers and included 1,531 responses. Freddie Mac's *Research Brief* stated that applicants who were subsequently approved for a mortgage stated they were initially denied for reasons later found to be quick fixes, such as appraisal differences or missing documentation. Many borrowers were subsequently approved after gathering the necessary funds or documents needed, and 76% of resubmissions were approved by the same lender.[57]

How to Submit a Complaint to the CFPB

The Consumer Financial Protection Bureau (CFPB) received approximately 27,900 mortgage complaints in 2023, according to the March 2024 *Consumer Response Annual Report*. The majority of mortgage-related complaints dealt with conventional mortgages (58%), followed by FHA mortgages (14%), and VA mortgages (9%). In 91% of instances, consumers attempted resolution before filing a complaint with the CFPB.[58]

Each week, the CFPB sends about 25,000 complaints about financial products and services to companies for response, and most companies respond within 15 days. The CFPB complaint site provides a video for consumers to see how the complaint process works, along with tools to search for answers. Complaints are processed for a dozen different types of financial products, including mortgages.

To watch the video, learn more, or submit a complaint, visit www.consumerfinance.gov/complaint/

CHAPTER 4

Discrimination & Redlining

ONE HUNDRED TWENTY-TWO MILLION DOLLARS HAS BEEN SECURED by the United States Department of Justice (DOJ) in settlements from twelve financial institutions across the nation who avoided and neglected to offer mortgage services to majority-Black and Hispanic neighborhoods. Enforcement actions were completed under the *Combatting Redlining Initiative,* launched by the Justice Department on October 22, 2021. The initiative represents the nations most aggressive and coordinated civil rights enforcement effort to eradicate redlining.

The majority of the $122 million—which was secured in just over two years—is allocated for loan subsidy funds to help support over 7,000 people in the impacted communities. The settlements also require the lenders to establish full-service branches in majority-Black and Hispanic neighborhoods, assign loan officers to serve those communities, and meet other conditions related to inclusive lending outreach.[59]

Historical Redlining

Redlining is the practice of denying people access to credit because of where they live, even if they personally qualify for a loan. Redlining took its roots in 1934 with the creation of the Federal Housing Administration (FHA), an agency tasked with insuring loans as part of an overhaul of the mortgage financing system decimated by the Depression. FHA determined that loans could not be economically sound if the property was located in a neighborhood that was—or could become—populated by Black people.[60]

The Home Owners' Loan Corporation (HOLC) was created under President Franklin D. Roosevelt's *New Deal* to increase homeownership for working-class Americans, as well as refinance mortgages for homeowners affected by the *Great Depression*. HOLC created a color-coded grading system to assess the desirability of residential communities, and categorized neighborhoods based on its racial, ethnic, and immigrant composition. Lines were drawn around neighborhoods on urban maps, rated on a scale of A to D, with color codes as follows: green for the "best," blue for "still desirable," yellow for "definitely declining," and red for "hazardous."[61]

The Fair Housing Act of 1968 banned discrimination in real estate and mortgage lending, including racially motivated redlining. By 1971, the Federal Reserve Board required the banks that it regulated to post Equal Housing Lender information in its lobbies.

In its study, *Redlining and Neighborhood Health*, the National Community Reinvestment Coalition (NCRC), stated "There is a higher prevalence of COVID-19 risk factors in historically redlined neighborhoods. The history of redlining, segregation and disinvestment not only reduced minority wealth, it impacted health and longevity, resulting in a legacy of chronic disease and premature death in many high minority neighborhoods. With the ongoing pandemic, the indication of greater risk factors for COVID-19 compounds the disparities in communities that have a history of redlining. Redlining and disinvestment are not only associated with greater segregation and economic inequality, but with the most basic attributes of public health, life expectancy and social vulnerability."[62]

Table 13 summarizes different forms of discrimination. Descriptions align with the fair lending examination guidelines of financial supervisory agencies.

TABLE 13 - FORMS OF DISCRIMINATION

Redlining	When an institution provides unequal access to credit within a geographic area based on an applicant's race, color, national origin, or prohibited characteristic. This type is also referred to as historical redlining.
Modern-Day Redlining	Activities, policies, and practices of an institution, including location of branches, advertising efforts, and where loan officers are placed. On the surface, activities appear to not discriminate—but have a discriminatory effect.
Digital Redlining	Marketing techniques based on algorithms used to select audiences in digital advertisements. Activities can exclude minorities, due to on-line advertising or social media campaigns that exclude protect class populations.
Reverse Redlining	Reverse redlining refers to the practice of targeting minority borrowers or targeting certain geographic areas with products or services that are less advantageous to the customer.
Disparate Impact Unintentional Bias	Occurs when a facially neutral policy or practice burdens certain persons on a prohibited basis. On the surface no one is expressly excluded, however the lender's standards are found to disproportionally exclude protected groups. Because there is no actual intent to discriminate, disparate impact is considered *unintentional*.
Disparate Treatment Intentional Bias	Disparate treatment is found when members of a protected group (when compared with white applicants with similar transaction characteristics) were charged higher loan costs, less favorable loan terms, or approved with stricter underwriting conditions. Disparate treatment is generally a regular practice rather than an isolated instance and considered *intentional*.

Modern-day Redlining

While historical redlining was considered an explicit, legally recognized course of action, modern-day redlining looks at the activities, policies, and practices of lenders. On the surface, activities appear to not discriminate—but have a discriminatory effect. According to the Department of Justice, "Modern-day redlining takes into account the location of retail branches, advertising efforts, and where loan officers are placed. Lenders are considered to be in violation of federal laws by avoiding potential loan applicants who reside in majority-minority census tracts, known as MMTs or MMCTs."[63]

The CFPB considers modern-day redlining to be "exclusionary conduct" by mortgage lenders—including nonbanks. The CFPB has stated, "When a lender either excludes protected groups of consumers from lending or targets those consumers with harmful credit products or services, they violate the Equal Credit Opportunity Act and potentially other consumer financial protection and civil rights laws."

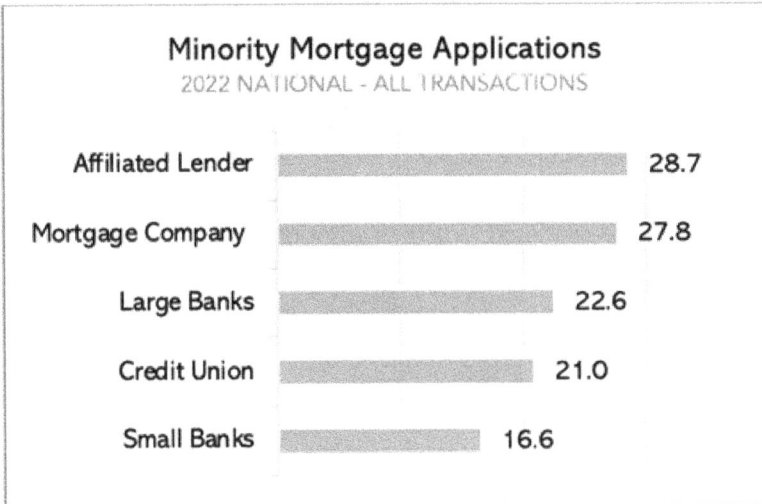

Minority Mortgage Applications
2022 NATIONAL - ALL TRANSACTIONS

Lender Type	Value
Affiliated Lender	28.7
Mortgage Company	27.8
Large Banks	22.6
Credit Union	21.0
Small Banks	16.6

TABLE 14 - Source: CFPB, Data Point: 2022 Mortgage Market Activity and Trends

DOJ & CFPB enforcement applies to both depository and non-depository lenders. Table 14 indicates the share of mortgage applications submitted by minority borrowers in 2022 by institution type. Affiliated lenders, which are bank-owned companies, had the largest share of applications, followed by independent mortgage companies. Depository institutions consist of large banks, credit unions, and small banks.

Digital Redlining

Digital redlining is a form of modern-day redlining and can result from any type of on-line advertising or social media campaign that excludes minority populations. Artificial intelligence programs based on algorithms that determine the recipients of digital advertisements can result in bias. The DOJ and CFPB consider any program to be discriminatory if minorities or protected classes are excluded from viewing the advertisements.

According to a joint study completed by the Federal Reserve Bank of New York and the Federal Reserve Bank of Philadelphia, financial technology, known as "fintech," companies are taking the lead in reaching underserved consumers. Known for having caused a digital disruption in the market, the fintech landscape has expanded quickly due to big data, data analytics, decisioning algorithms, and artificial intelligence. Fintech firms target nonprime consumers, including people who have been denied or filed for bankruptcy, which enable alternative lenders to reach vulnerable populations.[64]

Reverse Redlining

Reverse redlining refers to the practice of targeting minority borrowers (or another protected class) or targeting certain geographic areas with products or services that are less advantageous to the customer. According to the CFPB, "Redlining is the practice of financial institutions not lending to certain groups, neighborhoods, or parts of a community. Discriminatory targeting involves targeting predatory products or practices to those communities, and has also been called reverse redlining, when targeting is on the basis of geography."[65]

The Justice Department, along with the CFPB, filed its first-ever reverse redlining case against a Texas-based developer and lender for operating an illegal land sales scheme and targeting tens of thousands of Hispanic borrowers with false statements and predatory loans. Foreclosures were initiated on 30% of the lots within three years of the purchase date, and 40% of the properties were purchased and resold, known as flipping. The "bait-and- switch" scam lured and exploited victims through Spanish-language social media posts and Tik-Tok.[66]

Equal Credit Opportunity Act

The Equal Credit Opportunity Act (ECOA) is the strongest civil rights law to protect consumers in the financial marketplace. As stated earlier in Chapter 3, ECOA prohibits lenders from discriminating against credit applicants on the basis of race, color, religion, national origin, sex, marital status, age, whether they are a recipient of public assistance, and whether they have exercised their rights under the Consumer Credit Protection Act.[67]

A creditor may inquire about the race, color, religion, national origin, or sex of an applicant or any other person—but an applicant is not required to provide the information. For government monitoring purposes, creditors are permitted to collect certain demographic information based on surname or visual observation. Under ECOA, a creditor cannot refuse to evaluate an applicant if their income is derived from part-time employment, alimony, child support, separate maintenance, annuity, pension or retirement benefit—but may consider the amount and probable continuance of the income.

(The full text of the ECOA Regulation is included in Chapter 13)

Community Reinvestment Act

The Community Reinvestment Act (CRA) was signed into law in 1977 and requires depository institutions to meet the credit needs of its community, particularly in low- and moderate-income areas. Products and services must align with the population demographics of the community.

Illinois, New York, and Massachusetts have enacted CRA laws for nonbanks, and Connecticut's CRA law applies to credit unions. Legislature is pending in California and Pennsylvania, and under review by other states.

Federal regulators have completed an extensive overhaul of CRA with stricter requirements which went into effect April 1, 2024, with key mandates effective January 1, 2026. Every 4 or 5 years, CRA examinations are completed by a supervisory agency, and banks are assigned a CRA rating as follows: outstanding, satisfactory, needs to improve, or substantial noncompliance. The CRA rating of any bank can be found on the FFIEC website at www.FFIEC.gov/craratings/

Fair Housing Act Updated Rule

The Fair Housing Act, passed as part of the Civil Rights Act of 1968, prohibits discrimination in housing-related transactions based on race, color, national origin, religion, sex, familial status, and disability. Housing-related transactions include any person who is in the business of selling, brokering, appraising, or lending money on real property.

On March 17, 2023, the Department of Housing and Urban Development (HUD) announced the restoration of the *Discriminatory Effects Standard*, a rule implemented under the Fair Housing Act. The Standard applies to any creditor, its officers, agents, or employees in granting or fixing the terms of credit. The regulation prohibits practices of housing-related activities which cause systemic inequality in housing, regardless of whether they were adopted with discriminatory intent.[68] The ruling pertains to disparate impact, a practice that occurs when a facially neutral policy burdens certain persons on a prohibited basis. Facially neutral means that—on the surface, or face value—no one is expressly excluded, however the lender's standards are found to disproportionally exclude protected groups.

(The full text of Fair Housing Act rules pertaining to real estate transactions is included in Chapter 14.)

Where to File a Complaint

USA.gov - general resource site

Consumers can report any type of discrimination or deceptive practices.

www.usa.gov/mortgage-company-complaints/

Phone 1-844-USAGOV1

Federal Trade Commission

Consumers can report a mortgage lender for deceptive practices, false statements about their ability to offer a loan, fees for services they didn't provide, illegal tactics to collect on mortgage balances, and mortgage relief scams.

www.reportfraud.ftc.gov

(See also: Chapter 3, How to submit a complaint to the CFPB, and Chapter 5, PAVE Get Help tools, report discrimination to HUD)

State Laws to Protect Consumers

Many states in the U.S. adopt consumer protection laws that are enforceable in conjunction with federal regulations. State-enacted fair housing laws set forth prohibited practices based on a person's race or religion, or other "protected class" in housing-related transactions. A protected class applies to individuals whose demographic characteristics are considered a "prohibited basis" under the Equal Credit Opportunity Act, Fair Housing Act, or other civil rights law.

State laws define which protected classes are included—and what types of discriminatory actions are prohibited—in relation to federal laws. In most cases, state legislation expands upon federal laws, thereby strengthening consumer rights. As an example, many states have expanded discrimination based on sex to also include sexual orientation and gender identity.

Table 15 on the following page denotes four categories of legislation that apply to protected classes. Categories in the table are explained below.

- ## Expanded laws
  Yes = certain fair housing protections have been adopted.

- ## Ancestry
  Yes = considered a protected class by the state and may not be used as a factor for housing related discrimination.

- ## Income source
  Yes = considered a protected class by the state and may not be used as a factor for housing related discrimination.

- ## LGBTQ+
  Yes = considered a protected class by the state and may not be used as a factor for housing related discrimination. Limited = law does not include gender identity or other LGBTQ+ distinction.[69]

	TABLE 15 – STATE FAIR HOUSING PROTECTIONS Laws Adopted for Protected Classes			
	Expanded Laws	Ancestry	Income Source	LGBTQ+
Alabama	Yes	Yes	No	No
Alaska	Yes	No	No	No
Arizona	Yes	No	No	No
Arkansas	Yes	No	No	Yes
California	Yes	Yes	Yes	Yes
Colorado	Yes	Yes	No	Yes
Connecticut	Yes	Yes	Yes	Yes
Delaware	Yes	No	Yes	Yes
District of Columbia	Yes	No	Yes	Yes
Florida	Yes	No	No	Limited
Georgia	Yes	No	No	Yes
Hawaii	Yes	No	No	Yes
Idaho	Yes	No	No	No
Illinois	Yes	Yes	No	Yes
Indiana	Yes	No	No	No
Iowa	Yes	No	No	No
Kansas	Yes	Yes	No	Limited
Kentucky	Yes	No	No	Limited
Louisiana	Yes	No	No	No
Maine	Yes	Yes	Yes	Yes
Maryland	Yes	No	No	Yes
Massachusetts	Yes	Yes	Yes	Yes
Michigan	No	Yes	No	Yes
Minnesota	Yes	Yes	Yes	Yes
Mississippi	Yes	No	No	No
Missouri	Yes	Yes	No	No
Montana	Yes	Yes	No	No
Nebraska	Yes	No	No	Limited
Nevada	Yes	Yes	No	Yes
New Hampshire	Yes	No	No	Yes
New Jersey	Yes	Yes	Yes	Yes
New Mexico	Yes	Yes	No	Yes
New York	Yes	Yes	Yes	Yes
North Carolina	Yes	No	No	No
North Dakota	Yes	No	Yes	Limited
Ohio	Yes	Yes	No	Limited
Oklahoma	Yes	No	Yes	No
Oregon	Yes	Yes	Yes	Yes
Pennsylvania	Yes	Yes	No	Limited
Rhode Island	Yes	Yes	No	Yes
South Carolina	Yes	No	No	No
South Dakota	Yes	Yes	No	No
Tennessee	Yes	Yes	No	No
Texas	Yes	No	No	No
Utah	Yes	Yes	Yes	Yes
Vermont	Yes	No	Yes	Yes
Virginia	Yes	No	No	Limited
Washington	Yes	Yes	No	Yes
West Virginia	Yes	Yes	No	No
Wisconsin	Yes	Yes	No	Limited
Wyoming	Yes	No	No	No

Sources: The Policy Surveillance Program (expanded laws); Foothold Technology (LGBTQ+)

CHAPTER 5

Appraisal Bias

OVER ONE HUNDRED SEVENTY THOUSAND HOMES were appraised below the home purchase contract price in 2023, according to the Federal Housing Finance Agency's Appraisal Gap Dashboard.[70] The undervaluation of property appraisals is a major cause of mortgage denials throughout the nation—particularly in areas with higher minority populations.

Table 16 shows the national count of below-contract appraisals, segmented by minority population level. The share of undervalued appraisals is 8.17% in 0–50% minority tracts, 10.57% in 50.01–80% minority tracts, and 13.35% in census tracts with 80.1–100% minority population.[71]

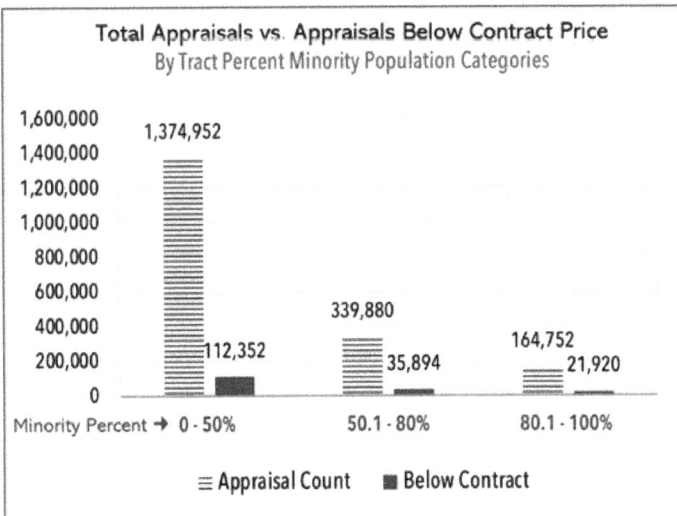

Total Appraisals vs. Appraisals Below Contract Price
By Tract Percent Minority Population Categories

Minority Percent	Appraisal Count	Below Contract
0 - 50%	1,374,952	112,352
50.1 - 80%	339,880	35,894
80.1 - 100%	164,752	21,920

≡ Appraisal Count   ■ Below Contract

TABLE 16 - Source: FHFA, Uniform Appraisal Dataset Aggregate Statistics, National 2023

Table 17 lists the 2023 median appraisal valuation for each U.S. state, along with the percent of appraisals which were above the contract price, equal to the contract price, and below the contract price.[72] Figures are based on the Federal Housing Finance Agency's UAD Aggregate Statistics State Dashboard, which can be accessed at www.fhfa.gov/datatools/tools/.

TABLE 17 – APPRAISAL VALUATIONS FOR HOME PURCHASES				
	Median Value	% Above Contract	% Equal to Contract	% Below Contract
Alabama	280 K	75	18.9	6
Alaska	395 K	57	33.8	9
Arizona	545 K	67	22.8	10
Arkansas	265 K	72	19.1	12
California	724 K	45	46	9
Colorado	575 K	67	21.1	6
Connecticut	393 K	58	39.1	10
Delaware	420 K	70	22.6	8
District of Columbia	815 K	69	25.8	5
Florida	425 K	69	19.7	7
Georgia	381 K	72	19	9
Hawaii	952 K	55	35.9	9
Idaho	441 K	74	19.5	6
Illinois	296 K	58	34.6	7
Indiana	260 K	66	25.2	9
Iowa	235 K	71	25.6	3
Kansas	261 K	67	25.7	7
Kentucky	265 K	71	23.3	6
Louisiana	255 K	77	15.9	7
Maine	373 K	71	18.6	11
Maryland	435 K	64	26	10
Massachusetts	600 K	57	36.2	7
Michigan	250 K	60	26.7	14
Minnesota	350 K	70	25	5
Mississippi	246 K	75	15.6	10
Missouri	270 K	71	22	7
Montana	462 K	71	23	6
Nebraska	280 K	65	28.4	6
Nevada	455 K	59	30	11
New Hampshire	477 K	63	23.1	13
New Jersey	510 K	55	33.5	11
New Mexico	333 K	68	20.7	11
New York	480 K	60	34.1	6
North Carolina	385 K	73	18.5	9
North Dakota	285 K	74	18.4	7
Ohio	247 K	64	25.9	10
Oklahoma	251 K	71	18.3	11
Oregon	510 K	68	27	5
Pennsylvania	295 K	65	25.3	10
Rhode Island	430 K	60	30.8	9
South Carolina	348 K	76	17.4	7
South Dakota	305 K	81	15.1	4
Tennessee	372 K	75	18.6	7
Texas	375 K	75	17.2	8
Utah	520 K	74	19.9	6
Vermont	392 K	70	16.7	14
Virginia	428 K	70	21	9
Washington	620 K	57	38	5
West Virginia	225 K	77	14.2	9
Wisconsin	298 K	66	24.4	10
Wyoming	345 K	68	26.5	5

Source: FHFA, Uniform Appraisal Dataset Aggregate Statistics, 2023

Racial Disparities in Appraisal Valuations

On March 13, 2023, The United States Justice Department filed a statement of interest to the U.S. District Court of Maryland alleging that an appraiser and a lender violated the Fair Housing Act and the Equal Credit Opportunity Act by lowering the valuation of a home because the owners were Black.[73]

The mortgage was denied on a refinance application based on an appraisal of $475,000. The owners, both university professors, were at home with their children when the home was appraised. The lender refused to respond to a letter from the owners which pointed out certain appraisal errors. After applying with a new lender and replacing their photos with images of White people, the home was appraised for $750,000.[74]

"Mortgage lenders can be held liable under federal law for relying upon discriminatory appraisals from third-party appraisers."

—U.S. Department of Justice

The FHFA commentary, *Reducing Valuation Bias by Addressing Appraiser and Property Valuation,* stated, "Appraisals are to be fair and free of bias, providing a supported value for a family's future or current home that reflects respect and equal treatment of the community and neighborhood in which the home is located."[75]

The FHFA stated that in its review of appraisals, they observed references to race and ethnicity in the "neighborhood description" and other free-form text fields in appraisal reports, citing overt references to race, ethnicity, and other descriptions indicating the presence of valuation bias. Concerns have arisen over possible inaccuracies and inequities in mortgage appraisals, with reports of low appraised values for Black homeowners replaced with much higher ones after a re-appraisal conducted with a white stand-in.[76]

Unacceptable Appraisal Practices

In January 2024, Fannie Mae and Freddie Mac separately issued updates to rules regarding unacceptable appraisal practices. Each enterprise provided a list of subjective terms and descriptions, and both enterprises stated they will not accept appraisal reports containing the listed phrases or discriminatory references to any protected class.

Unacceptable practices include the appraiser's consideration of the race, color, religion, sex, sexual orientation, gender identity, age, marital status, disability, familial status, exercise of any federally protected civil right, receipt of income derived from any public assistance program, birthplaces of residents at the property or in the neighborhood, national origin of the prospective owners or occupants of the subject property or of the present owners or occupants of the properties in the vicinity of the subject property.

The use of unsupported assumptions, interjections of personal opinion, or perceptions and the use of subjective terminology are prohibited. A small sampling of unacceptable phraseology used to describe properties or locations include the following: good or bad location, desirable or undesirable, pride of ownership (or no pride), gentrified, working class, inner city, up and coming, and preferred community. Also included in the extensive listing of unacceptable terms are references to Millennials, Generation X, or Baby Boomers.[77]

Automated Valuation Models and Hybrid Appraisals

Automated valuation models (AVMs) are statistically based computer programs that use real estate information to estimate property values. AVMs provide fast and easy access to property valuations; however, federal agencies have cautioned the mortgage industry regarding discriminatory risks in the use of AVMs.

On June 1, 2023, six federal agencies issued a proposed rule regarding automated valuation models to address the algorithmic and computational models used to assess the value of homes. New AVM standards would require mortgage lenders to adopt and maintain policies and other safeguards to ensure greater confidence in valuation estimates, protect against data manipulation, avoid conflicts of interest and discrimination.[78]

Hybrid appraisals are a streamlined and cost-saving option that combines the traditional appraisal process with data-driven technology. There are two roles involved in a hybrid appraisal, and they can be completed by more than one person. One role serves as the collector of property and market data, and the other role is evaluating the interior and exterior of the home. Under Fannie Mae and Freddie Mac rules, hybrid appraisals are permissible on certain transactions and must also meet specific underwriting criteria.

Right to Receive Free Copy of Appraisal

The Equal Credit Opportunity Act (ECOA) requires mortgage lenders to provide applicants with free copies of appraisals and other written valuations. The law applies to all first-lien mortgages and certain higher-cost mortgages. Within three business days after submitting a loan application, lenders must issue a notification to borrowers explaining their right to receive a report.

Copies of appraisals must be sent promptly after the lender's receipt of the report, or three business days prior to loan closing—whichever is earlier. Appraisals can be delivered by hand, by email, or sent by mail, as long as it is received by the borrower three full business days prior to closing. Under this law, Saturday is not counted as a business day. If appraisals are delivered via email, the lender must comply with the consumer consent provisions of the Electronic Signatures in Global and National Commerce Act (E-Sign Act).

Reconsideration of Value

People who are purchasing a home—as well as homeowners who are refinancing their mortgage—can ask their lender for a reconsideration of value (ROV) if they believe their property appraisal contains inaccurate information or if the appraisal was influenced by bias.

On June 8, 2023, five federal banking agencies issued proposed guidance concerning the rights for consumers to request an ROV. Rules will require institutions to establish a process requiring appraisers and other involved entities to reassess the value of a home. On May 1, 2024, mandatory requirements for lenders to have policies and procedures for ROVs were announced to HUD, Fannie Mae and Freddie Mac.[79]

To request an ROV, borrowers need to point out errors or omissions or inadequate comparable properties, and/or provide evidence of bias. According to the CFPB, deficient collateral valuations can contain inaccuracies due to errors, omissions, or discrimination that affect the value conclusion. The proposed guidance aims to help institutions identify, address, and mitigate valuation discrimination risk.[80]

Property Appraisal and Valuation Equity (PAVE) Task Force

The Interagency Task Force for Property Appraisal and Valuation Equity (PAVE) was established in 2021 to evaluate the causes, extent, and consequences of appraisal bias and to establish a transformative set of recommendations to root out racial and ethnic bias in home valuations.

PAVE consists of 13 federal agencies, who engage with philanthropic organizations, civil rights leaders, academics, housing industry stakeholders, and everyday Americans who currently own, or aspire to own, a home.[81]

The CFPB serves on the PAVE Task Force, as well as the FFIEC's Appraisal Subcommittee (ASC) who provide federal oversight of state appraiser and appraisal management company regulatory programs. ASC serves as a monitoring framework to protect public policy interests in real estate appraisals and administers the Appraisal Complaint National Hotline.[82]

The PAVE Action Plan aims to empower consumers to take action against appraisal bias. "Consumers who seek to finance to refinance a home are often unaware of their options when they receive a lower-than-expected valuation, according to HUD."

In January 2023, HUD published guidance to make it easier and quick for prospective borrowers applying for a Federal Housing Administration (FHA)-insured loan to request a Reconsideration of Value (ROV) on a property if the initial valuation is lower because of suspected illegal bias.

PAVE has taken steps to remove unnecessary educational and experience requirements that make it difficult for underrepresented groups to access the profession and to strengthen anti-bias, fair housing, and fair lending training of existing appraisers. In January 2023, the Department of Veterans Affairs (VA) released new guidance to its appraiser workforce.[83]

PAVE's Get Help Tools for Consumers

PAVE administers a robust website for consumers to find information and assistance. From the home page (pave.hud.gov) users can select "Get Help" and proceed through a series of actionable steps to appeal an undervalued appraisal or to report housing discrimination. Applicable web links and telephone numbers are included.

- Reconsideration of value
  Infographics explain the reconsideration of value (ROV) process and provides guidance for requesting an ROV from the mortgage lender.

- Report housing discrimination
Housing discrimination can be reported on-line through PAVE's submission process. Investigations are completed by HUD's Office of Fair Housing and Equal Opportunity (FHEO).

- Report inappropriate appraiser conduct
The housing discrimination page also includes information for reporting inappropriate conduct to the Appraisal Subcommittee (ASC).

FFIEC Statement on Valuation Discrimination

February 12, 2024, the Federal Financial Institutions Examination Council (FFIEC) issued a *Statement on Examination Principles Related to Valuation Discrimination and Bias in Residential Lending*. The statement was issued to communicate principles for the examination of the appraisal and evaluation practices to financial institutions who are supervised by a regulatory agency.

The FFIEC Statement outlines risks from valuation discrimination and bias and warns institutions that failure of internal controls to identify, monitor, and control valuation discrimination or bias could negatively affect credit decisions. The FFIEC stated that noncompliance with laws and regulations can negatively affect assessment of an institution's management in a supervisory safety and soundness examination.[84]

HUD–NAREB Partnership to Combat Appraisal Bias

August 2, 2023, the Department of Housing and Urban Development (HUD) announced a partnership with the National Association of Real Estate Brokers (NAREB) to address appraisal bias and discrimination. The collaboration between HUD and NAREB aim to increase understanding of appraisal bias in specific geographic areas, collaborate on efforts to combat appraisal bias, and share best practices for housing counselors.

The initiative includes training sessions and discussion of strategies to combat appraisal bias; best practices for housing counselors to help clients impacted; and available resources that can support housing counselors and their clients. HUD's Office of Housing Counseling and National Fair Housing Training Academy works with NAREB in roundtables across the country to gain greater understanding of appraisal bias in specific geographic areas; build public-private partnerships and collaboration in efforts to combat appraisal bias; and share best practices for housing counselors to help impacted clients.[85]

Uniform Standards of Professional Appraisal Practice (USPAP)

USPAP was adopted by Congress in 1989 and is the recognized ethical and performance standards entity for the appraisal profession in the U.S. Compliance to USPAP principles is required for state-licensed and state-certified appraisers involved in federally related transactions, such as loans sold to Fannie Mae, Freddie Mac, and loans insured by a government agency.

The universal form utilized by residential mortgage lenders is known as the Uniform Residential Appraisal Report (URAR). USPAP requires that, upon completing the URAR, appraisers must certify that they did not base, either partially or completely, the analysis and/or opinion of market value in the appraisal report on the race, color, religion, sex, age, marital status, handicap, familial status, or national origin of either the prospective owners or occupants of the subject property or of the present owners or occupants of the properties in the vicinity of the subject property, or on any other basis prohibited by law.[86]

CHAPTER 6

Innovative Solutions

HOMEOWNERSHIP IS WITHIN REACH FOR EVEN MORE PEO-PLE, thanks to innovative mortgage programs and flexible qualifying rules. For those with minimal credit history or no credit score, there are mortgage programs that accept alternative forms of credit verification. Well known credit agencies have built score-building technology to help consumers strengthen their credit profile for buying a home. Mortgage lenders offer streamlined documentation options for self-employed borrowers, noncitizens, and people with little or no banking experience.

Non-QM Mortgages

The most popular innovative financing programs are known as "non-QM" loans, which are mortgages with terms and features not permitted under the federally-mandated Qualified Mortgage (QM) rule. Mortgages that are sold to government-sponsored enterprises (GSEs) such as Fannie Mae or Freddie Mac, and loans insured by government agencies such as FHA, VA, or USDA Rural Housing must adhere to QM rules.

"The share of non-qualified mortgages doubled from 2020 to 2022. Though the non-QM loan is a small piece of today's mortgage market, it plays a key role in meeting the credit needs for homebuyers not able to obtain financing through the GSE or government channels."[87]

—Core Logic

In 2022, almost 55% of the non-QM borrowers used limited or alternative documentation, according to Core Logic. The average credit score was 771, compared to 776 for homebuyers with QM loans and 714 for government loans. The average LTV for borrowers for non-QMs was 76%, compared to 77% for QMs. The average debt-to-income ratio was 37% for non-QMs and 33% for QM loans.[88]

Lenders often introduce a non-QM option to borrowers who are not able to provide the standard paperwork needed for a conforming mortgage. Because documentation is more streamlined, loans can be approved faster, which is advantageous in getting a home at a good price.

Some people follow the adage, "buy now—refinance later" when interest rates are high. Once settled into a new home, people can start building wealth—and at the same time—start building a strong credit history through timely mortgage payments. In the future, they would likely to be eligible for "prime rate" refinancing.

Higher interest rates can potentially be offset by the growth in real estate value. For example, a two-percent higher rate (6.00% vs. 4.00%) will cost about $2,400 more each year for a $200,000 mortgage. Based on a growth rate of 6% per year, a home valued at $200,000 would be worth $12,000 more at the end of 12 months. The loan may cost an extra $200 each month, but the equity in the home is building at the rate of $1,000 each month.

The above example is simplified for clarity. Non-QM interest rates are tiered for each loan program option, and pricing typically starts at 1% over prime. Other parameters such as loan-to-value, owner-occupancy, and credit scores are factored into loan pricing.

Many non-QM options stretch DTI ratios to 55%, versus the QM standard which is 43%. There are programs that accept credit scores as low as 500 and borrowers with a recent bankruptcy.

The most streamlined non-QM program is known as "NINA," which is an acronym for a "no income—no asset" mortgage. Non-QM loans are also called non-conforming, non-prime, or non-agency. A number of programs offered by nationwide lenders are described on the following pages.

Asset-based Loans

Also referred to as an "asset depletion loan," borrowers can leverage their assets to qualify for a mortgage. Acceptable assets include retirement accounts, investment accounts, or other liquid sources. Qualifying is usually based on 70% or 80% of the account value. Ideally suited for retired people, monthly income from Social Security or other source is added to qualifying figures. The major difference among loan programs is very important—some require assets to be pledged, and others do not require assets to be pledged.

Bank Statement Loans

Self-employed borrowers can obtain a mortgage based on the income shown on checking account statements in lieu of tax returns. Bank statement loans are a popular non-QM program, and options vary widely among lenders. Loan approval is based on the monthly average of deposits over a period of time. The number of months' bank statements requested by the lender can range from 2 to 12 months.

Foreign National and ITIN Mortgages

Individual Tax Identification Numbers (ITINs) are used in lieu of a social security number. There are some mortgage programs that accept a VISA or VISA waiver in lieu of an ITIN. Credit history and verification steps vary by lender and loan pricing is generally structured according to the percent of down payment, property type, and occupancy. Credit scores and credit history requirements are usually flexible to accommodate foreign nationals with limited credit. Some programs require applicants to submit two years' federal tax returns and provide documentation to verify cash assets used for the down payment and closing costs.

Recent Credit Event Loans

A viable option for people who have recently experienced financial hardship, recent credit event loans will accept recent foreclosures or bankruptcies. Although conforming loans will accept loans from borrowers who have filed bankruptcy, the most lenient rule is for FHA loans, which requires a two-year waiting period after a bankruptcy discharge.

1099 Income Loans

Ideally suited for independent contractors and free-lancers, mortgage approval is based on income reported on 1099 forms issued by clients. The 1099 program is an alternative to federal tax returns, and mortgage approval is based on gross receipts—business expenses are not factored into qualifying figures.

P&L Loans

Another streamlined option for self-employed borrowers, P&L loans (profit and loss) do not require bank statements or federal tax returns. Qualifying income is calculated from statements prepared by a Certified Public Accountant or other licensed tax agent. For example, if a borrower owns a company that has $180,000 in revenue, and business expenses amount to $60,000, the P&L will indicate a $120,000 net profit. Mortgage approval is based on $10,000 monthly income.

Special Purpose Credit Programs

Special purpose credit programs, known as SPCPs, are financing programs available from banks that are required to serve lower-income communities in compliance with the Community Reinvestment Act. SPCPs enable bank customers to finance a home purchase with affordable repayment terms, flexible underwriting, and minimal cash investment. In June 2022, the CFPB issued an official statement for lenders to increase credit access to better serve historically disadvantages individuals and communities. Loans must be structured to benefit people who would otherwise be denied credit or receive it on less favorable terms.[89]

Halal Mortgage Options for Muslims

There are several types of financial options for Muslims and individuals in need of faith-based financing. Both purchase and refinancing solutions are available from various companies that adhere to Islamic financing guidelines. Loans are Sharia-compliant and riba-free, which means interest is not charged on the loan. The three common types of Halal mortgages are Ijara, Musharaka, and Murabaha.[90]

Solutions for Unbanked Loan Applicants

Buying a home and obtaining a mortgage require consumers to have established checking and/or savings accounts with a depository institution. For noncitizens, mainstream banking is a challenge due to the lack of identifying documentation that is required to establish an account. According to a report by the Federal Deposit Insurance Corporation (FDIC), "An estimated 4.5% of U.S. households were unbanked" in 2021, meaning that no one in the household had a checking or savings account at a bank or credit union. This represents approximately 5.9 million U.S. households."[91]

By law, financial institutions must comply with customer identification program (CIP) requirements for a consumer to open a bank account, apply for a loan, or obtain a credit card. Banks must also comply with the Bank Secrecy Act (BSA) and the USA Patriot Act, requiring the collection and verification of a person's name, date of birth, address, and identification number. For people born in the United States, their identification number would be either a Social Security Number (SSN) or a tax identification number (TIN).

Anyone who does not have a Social Security number, including immigrants, can apply for an individual taxpayer identification number (ITIN) from the Internal Revenue Service. According to the Federal Financial Institutions Examination Council (FFIEC), "Banks can make an exception for opening an account for someone who has applied for a tax identification number—but has not yet received it."[92]

Generally, more than one document is required to verify identity. Documents must have a photo and can include any of the following items: passport and country of issuance, alien identification number, Visa, or other U.S. immigration document, driver's license, employment authorization card, or school ID. Instructions on how to obtain an ITIN are available on the USA.gov site at www.usa.gov/itin/

Credit Score Booster Programs

The credit score was originally developed in the 1950s by a data analytics company called Fair Isaac Corporation.[30] Known as "FICO," the score was built and continues to be maintained by Fair Isaac's proprietary technology that analyzes consumer spending and other behaviors. The modelling technology of the FICO Score® produces a rating for each consumer that renders a credit score on a scale ranging from 300 to 850. People can build a credit profile through the applications featured below.

- UltraFICO Score®

    Consumers can build a credit profile with a smartphone app from Fair Isaac Corp. The UltraFICO® Score algorithm tracks checking and savings activity that strengthens a consumer's financial standing and broadens access to credit for young or immigrant applicants. www.fico.com

- Experian Boost™

    Consumers can set up on-going bill payment monitoring of any utility or service such as electricity, gas, landline or Cell Phone Company, cable TV, etc. paid from a bank account. As bills are paid timely, data is migrated to the consumer's credit report and their score is given an immediate boost. www.experian.com

No Credit Score or Limited History

According to a study by TransUnion completed in 2022, 45 million people in America are credit underserved. As one of the three major credit reporting agencies in the U.S., TransUnion released a global study that underscores the importance of financial inclusion. The study explains that *unserved* consists of consumers who have never had an open traditional credit product, and *underserved* are consumers with some—but limited—credit presence.[93]

Underserved consumers are disproportionately excluded from opening a credit card, buying a car, or obtaining a conventional or government-insured mortgage. They pay higher security deposits when renting an apartment or when they sign up for cable and internet service.

According to a report completed by the Oliver Wyman Company, *Financial Inclusion and Access to Credit*, people who have no mainstream credit file are considered "credit invisible," and accounted for about 28 million people in America in 2022. Another 21 million have limited information in their file, but not enough to generate a conventional credit score. This group of people are considered "unscorable."[94]

"26% of Hispanic consumers and 28% of Black consumers are credit invisible or unscorable, compared to 16% of White and Asian consumers."

—Oliver Wyman Corp.

Alternative Credit Options

Alternative sources of credit can be used for borrowers with no credit score or limited history. Such methods generally described as "non-traditional credit" and are acceptable for loans sold to Fannie Mae, Freddie Mac, and loans that are insured by FHA, VA, and USDA Rural Housing. A list of alternative credit sources is included in Chapter 9, Mortgage Approval Process.

CHAPTER 7

Down Payment Assistance

MORE THAN TWO THOUSAND PROGRAMS ARE AVAILABLE to help homebuyers across the nation. Down payment assistance (DPA) programs help people overcome the number one barrier to homeownership—cash to cover the down payment. Down payment assistance brings much-needed cash, expands mortgage affordability, and can reduce or altogether eliminate private mortgage insurance (PMI).

When shopping for a mortgage, it's wise to look at the "whole package" of what a lender has to offer. Home financing can be more advantageous when incentives are taken into account—even if the interest rate is a little higher.

Many DPA programs also help cover closing costs or finance certain property repairs. Table 18 illustrates five popular types of down payment assistance, explained on the following pages.

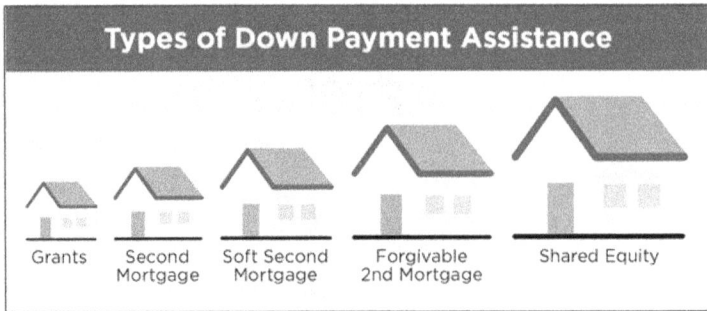

Types of Down Payment Assistance

Grants | Second Mortgage | Soft Second Mortgage | Forgivable 2nd Mortgage | Shared Equity

Table 18

Grants

Grants are like gifts since they are free and require no repayment. Amounts are modest, and typically less than $5,000. For the most part, grants are only available to first-time homebuyers purchasing owner-occupied properties and have maximum income restrictions. Grants are usually offered by local municipalities and administered by the city or town's housing division. With a grant, there is no lien on the property. Some grants include a covenant whereby a proportionate amount of money must be returned to the grantor if the home is sold within the first year or other time period.

In addition to first-time homebuyer grants, municipalities and housing partnership organizations offer grants for home improvement. Such grants may be limited to a specific purpose such as lead paint removal, energy improvements, or to construct handicap accessory features. Special grants are often available to active military personnel, or people who are employed within the municipality as a teacher, first responder, firefighter, law enforcement officer, or health care worker.

Second Mortgages

By definition, a second mortgage is a loan that is second in position under a first mortgage and referred to as a "subordinate lien" or a "junior lien." Loans are typically for 10- to 20-year terms and must be paid in full when the house is sold, or the first mortgage is refinanced. Second mortgages can be "zero percent," or they can be a low-interest "amortizing loan." Two popular repayment options are explained below.

"Deferred payment loans" are structured for repayment to begin after an initial period of time. Standard mortgage qualification rules exclude any debt payment that is not due for three years after loan closing. For that reason, payments on deferred payment loans often begin after 36 months.

"Step-payment" programs are formulated so that monthly payments increase on a gradual basis over a specified period of time. Typically, payments change in 3, 5, or 7 years, and some programs require no payments for an initial time period.

Soft Second Mortgages

Soft second mortgages are also called "silent seconds" because you don't realize the loan is there. There is no monthly payment, and loans are often at zero interest. For programs structured with interest, borrowers receive an amortization schedule delineating the projected loan balance at incremental points throughout the term. Many housing partnership agencies offer soft seconds up to 20% of the purchase price, eliminating the need for private mortgage insurance.

Forgivable Loans

Just as the name implies, all or part of the loan is "forgiven" over a certain period of time. The loan may be zero-percent or structured with interest, and for smaller loans there is usually no property lien. Typically, at the end of every 12-month period, a certain percentage of the loan balance is forgiven. As an example, a 3-year forgivable loan in the amount of $3,600 would be reduced to $2,400 balance owed at the end of 12 months and reduced to $1,200 after two years. At the end of the third year, the balance is zero. Forgivable loans are structured in many different ways and sometimes the forgivable feature begins after the homebuyer has lived in the home for at least one or two years.

Shared Equity

Financing assistance in the form of a shared equity agreement is generally offered by affordable housing developers to enable homeownership for people with no cash for a down payment. Most often, projects are completed in collaboration with a nonprofit or community development trust who serve as community stewards on a permanent basis. Homes are typically sold at 25% to 30% below market, and the investment agency may also subsidize first mortgage financing. Homebuyers must meet income eligibility guidelines based on the median income tables for the area. Homeowners are often invited to serve on operating boards or participate in community activities or support services. Three types of shared equity programs are summarized on the following page in Table 19.

Types of Shared Equity

Community Land Trust
- Trust owns the land and leases it to the homeowner
- Home is purchased for below-market value
- If owner sells home, a modest portion of the "increase" in value is shared with the trust

Shared Appreciation Loan
- Can be a first mortgage or a second mortgage
- Generally 20% of the purchase price is provided to buyer to use as down payment
- If home is sold, owner shares a portion of the increase in value (appreciation)

Deed Restriction
- Buyer obtains home at a discount from community investment partnership or municipal program
- Buyer agrees to a "restrictive re-sale deed" allowing agent to sell the home to an affordable household

Table 19

Downpayment Toward Equity Act of 2024

The Downpayment Toward Equity Act (H.R. 4231) is a bill that is pending with the 2023-2024 Congress that provides homebuyer grants up to $25,000. The Act was first introduced to the U.S. House of Representatives in 2021 by California Congresswoman Maxine Waters, the first woman and African American Chair of the House Financial Services Committee. A corresponding bill was introduced to the U.S. Senate by Georgia Senator Raphael Warnock on March 12, 2024.[95]

Status can be found by searching "HR 4231" at www.congress.gov

First Generation Downpayment Fund

The First Generation program was part of the "Build Back Better Act" passed by the U.S. House of Representatives in November, 2021. The $10 billion grant program is allocated to U.S. states and available through housing partnership organizations and other eligible entities. The program is available from participating housing finance agencies, explained further in Chapter 11. Summarized below are the key features of the program, as written in the Build Back Better Act.[96]

- Eligible recipients include first-time homebuyers who meet income requirements and qualify as what the Act terms as "first-generation" homebuyers.

- First-time homebuyers are those who have not owned a home in the prior three years.

- First-generation homebuyers are individuals whose parents or guardians never owned a home during the homebuyer's lifetime (excluding heir property) and whose spouse has not owned a home in the last three years. Any individual who has lived in foster care also qualifies as a first-generation homebuyer as long as they have not owned a home in the previous three years.

- Homebuyers must have an income at or below 120% of the area median income (AMI) for either the area where the home being purchased is located or the area where the homebuyer's place of residence is located. Income limits are increased to 140% of AMI if the home being purchased is located in a high-cost area.

- Homebuyers may receive the greatest of ten percent of the home's purchase price or $20,000. Assistance used to make a home accessible for those with disabilities are not counted in the maximum assistance amount. Amounts may be increased for qualified homebuyers who are economically disadvantaged.

- Funds can be used for the purchase of any home eligible for purchase by Fannie Mae or Freddie Mac, insurance by HUD, FHA, or USDA Rural Housing, or to benefit a military veteran.

Where to Find Grants and Downpayment Assistance

It's never too early to begin exploring where you can find free money. Even if buying a home is many months away, it is a worthwhile step to find out what resources are available. Across the nation, there are thousands of cities and towns that provide grants and financial assistance to new homebuyers as well as existing homeowners. In addition to locating a grant or some form of financial assistance for purchasing a home, people can learn what services and incentives are available after the home is purchased.

An important benefit to completing this research is learning about what the community is giving back to the people who live there.

Table 20 on the following page outlines tips for searching local websites for grants and down payment assistance. Summarized below are sources from national providers.

Freddie Mac DPA One

Freddie Mac administers a nationwide network that serves as a centralized resource of municipal, local, and state down payment assistance. www.dpaone.freddiemac.com

Fannie Mae

Down payment assistance ranging from $2,500 to $5,000 is available with certain Fannie Mae mortgage programs through authorized lenders.
www.HUD.gov/states

From the *State Information* landing page, choose any state, and proceed through each of the following menu options to locate resources:
Homeownership / Buying a home / Assistance programs

Down Payment Resource

More than 2,000 nationwide programs are tracked by Down Payment Resource, along with articles and helpful information for consumers.
www.downpaymentresource.com

TABLE 20 –MUNICIPAL GRANTS & DOWN PAYMENT ASSISTANCE	
Search Terms	Top Level Domain
Enter just a few key words for the desired property location from any web browser. For example: • first-time homebuyer • atlanta • georgia *For more results, broaden the search with name of county, parish, or general region.*	*Take note of the Top Level Domain (TLD)* .gov .state/us
After reaching the official site for a municipality, search to find programs using the key words: • homebuyer grants • homeowner grants • down payment assistance • first-time homebuyer • homeownership • affordable homebuyer	*Websites with the above TLDs indicate an office of the state or local government.*
After reaching a nonprofit or housing partnership organization, search for: • homebuyer grants • down payment assistance • soft seconds • first-time homebuyer • first-generation homebuyer • low-income homebuyer	.org *Websites with .org TLD are common for nonprofits and housing agencies.*
Note programs available to "homeowners or community residents" on municipal websites for incentives after purchasing the home: • energy-efficiency upgrades • insulation and weatherization • roof or window replacement • home water safety • lead paint removal • mitigation of mold, radon, or carbon monoxide • installation of handicap features	

CHAPTER 8

Find an Advocate

FOUR THOUSAND HUD-CERTIFIED HOUSING COUNSELORS are available across the nation through a network of 1,500 Housing Counseling Agencies (HCAs) administered by the Department of Housing and Urban Development (HUD). The HUD housing counseling program serves approximately 1 million clients each year, and every counselor is trained and certified by HUD.

Counseling agencies provide information, advice, and tools for people who are looking to find a home, need help with financing, maintaining the home, or other services. HUD's robust web portal enables consumers to locate and seek counseling services. The system's telephonic search capability offers translation services in more than 250 languages.[97]

Counseling is one-on-one assistance that addresses a home-buyer's unique circumstances and helps overcome specific obstacles to achieving a housing goal including (but not limited to) repairing credit, saving money for a down payment, qualifying for down payment assistance, and raising awareness about topics such as predatory lending practices. Counseling usually includes the creation of an action plan to meet the client's housing goals.[98]

Everyone needs an advocate when they are buying a home, especially first-time—or first-generation—homebuyers. Even for borrowers who have been pre-approved, finances are just part of the equation. Buying and financing a home involves many different service providers. A qualified counselor can serve as a trusted advisor, working to make sure that fair and impartial treatment is being extended uniformly by all parties.

According to HUD's report, *Housing Counseling Works: 2023 Update*, "Pre-purchase counseling may help individuals determine if they are ready for homeownership and connect them with safer, more affordable mortgage products." The report summarized findings from a study which analyzed perception bias toward total household debt and mortgage payments among low- to moderate-income first-time homebuyers who completed an online homebuyer education course. The study found that borrowers who underestimated their total debt of $5,000 or more took out larger mortgages with greater monthly payments.[99]

HUD Let's Make Home the Goal

HUD's Office of Housing Counseling (OHC) provides resource for first-time homebuyers, and works with housing counselors, local organizations, and community leaders across the country. The campaign was created to help more individuals and families with financial planning, getting a mortgage, and buying a home. HUD's *Let's Make Home the Goal* campaign is reaching cities across the U.S. to share homeownership opportunities and how HUD-certified housing counseling can help families reach their financial and homeownership goals.[100] Information and search tools to locate a housing counselor can be found at www.hud.gov/makehome-thegoal/

Find a HUD-certified Housing Counselor

The landing page from the *Let's Make Home the Goal* site provides users with the option of searching for a counselor by zip code, or to view the map and list for the entire state. Users can view all services provided by the agencies or choose a specific service from the following list of options:

- Bringing your mortgage current
- Buying a home
- Home improvement and repair services
- Homeless services
- Managing or budgeting your finances
- Rental housing services
- Reverse mortgage
- Your fair housing rights / file complaint

Users can view all options, or choose from the following:

- Face-to-face counseling
- Group counseling
- Internet counseling
- Phone counseling
- Video conference
- Other counseling

Users can view all languages or choose from the following:

- ASL
- Arabic
- Cambodian
- Cantonese
- Chinese Mandarin
- Creole
- Czech
- English
- Farsi
- French
- German
- Hindi
- Hmong
- Indonesian
- Italian
- Korean
- Polish
- Portuguese
- Russian
- Spanish
- Swahili
- Turkish
- Ukrainian
- Vietnamese

CFPB Homebuyer Tools

From the home page of the Consumer Financial Protection Bureau (CFPB) website, (consumerfinance.gov) users can select "consumer education," and choose "resources for yourself." The *Consumer Resources* landing page includes a section "educational tools you can use," which lists "buying a home," as well as other financing topics.

The *Buying a Home* landing page provides a full range of tools to guide consumers through the steps that include "before making an offer on a home," and "after making an offer." A printable 2-page "roadmap" can be used for planning each step. Various tools on the site include checklists for checking your credit, exploring interest rates, loan selection, understanding loan estimates, and how to understand closing forms.[101]

The CFPB counselor lookup tool—which is powered by HUD—is searchable by zip code and produces detailed (and printable) listing of all agencies near the selected area. A flash map displays the location of each agency, identified by a corresponding number from the list. Information for each agency includes:

- Description of all services provided
- List of all languages spoken
- # of miles from the selected zip code
- Street address
- Clickable links to agency website, email, and telephone.

The CFPB counselor lookup tool landing page is www.consumerfinance.gov/find-a-housing-counselor

Fannie Mae – Home View® Homebuyer Education Certificate

Fannie Mae Home View® is an on-line certificate course that aligns with national industry standards for pre-purchase homeownership education. The program fulfills the education requirements for most mortgage programs and is available in English and Spanish. After finishing the course and passing the quiz with a score of 80% or higher, participants receive a certificate of completion to share with their lender. Course modules are listed:

1. Knowing when you're ready.

2. Saving for homeownership.

3. Understanding the mortgage loan process.

4. Shopping for a home with a real estate agent.

5. Making an offer on a house.

6. Getting ready to close on your loan.

7. Welcome to homeownership!

Detailed information and additional resources can be found Fannie Mae's main website www.fanniemae.com. From the *Homebuyers, Owners, and Renters* landing page, select "buy" from the top menu. The site includes a range of tools to "prepare for the costs of buying and owning a home."[102]

Fannie Mae – Get Help from a Housing Counselor

Free personalized assistance is available for homebuyers and homeowners to help overcome financial uncertainty, disaster recovery, or other housing-related issues. Services are confidential and provided by nonprofit counseling partners in multiple languages.[103] Enter the search term "talk to a housing counselor" on the website www.yourhome.fanniemae.com, or call

1-855-HERE2HELP (855-437-3243)

Freddie-Mac – Credit Smart® Homebuyer U

Freddie Mac provides a course that can be completed using a phone app that offers a tailored experience with tools and trackers. Printable certificates can be delivered to a lender, housing professional, or co-borrower.[104] Lessons are available in English and Spanish, and cover the following topics:

1. Overview and introduction to the home buying process

2. Managing your money

3. Your credit and why it is important

4. Getting a mortgage

5. Finding a home and closing on a loan

6. Preserving homeownership

The site is located at creditsmart.freddiemac.com.

Freddie Mac -Borrower Help Centers

Freddie Mac administers a network of help centers where HUD-certified counselors provide assistance to prepare for successful homeownership. Help centers also provide assistance to homeowners who are struggling to make mortgage payments. On the site www.myhomefreddiemac.com, users can navigate to the page: getting help-working-with-housing-counselor.

The section "How to find a housing counselor" includes web links to other sites, including the CFPB, the national HOPE hotline. Counselors can be located from the link "Freddie Mac's Borrower Help Centers and Network." After selecting the geographical region (Midwest, Northeast, Southeast, Southwest, or West) the site produces a full detailed listing of agencies, along with clickable links to the agency's website. [105]

CHAPTER 9

Mortgage Approval Process

BORROWERS NEED TO BUILD A PICTURE OF STRENGTH demonstrating that they—along with any co-borrowers—can responsibly finance a home. Even though mortgage applications involve hundreds of digital images, and most processing steps are completed electronically, mortgage lenders ask borrowers for lots of paperwork. Known as "supporting documents," the information provided is needed to support loan approval.

Long before people begin their home buying journey, they can start to build their picture of strength by gathering paperwork related to income, cash assets, and paid bills. For example, overtime pay is listed on a paystub—but not on a W-2 tax form. In order to include OT as qualifying income, lenders will ask for paystubs. When meeting with a lender, being prepared with several months' financial history is a major advantage in moving along the approval process.

When mortgages are evaluated, lenders look at a number of factors—and each factor carries a certain amount of weight. Sometimes a loan application will have strength in one area, but weakness in another area. However, there is a chance the loan can be approved through a process known as "compensating factors."

As an example, if a borrower's debt-to-income ratio (DTI) is out-side the underwriting guideline—but the borrower has no debt—the DTI weakness is compensated by the strength of being debt-free. When credit history is weak, it can be compensated by a low DTI ratio, or a higher down payment.

Four Factors of Mortgage Qualification

The loan evaluation process looks at four factors: property and transaction, cash assets, borrower credit, and qualifying income. Each factor is explained.

Factor #1 - Property and Transaction

The property must conform to guidelines pertaining to legal zon-ing, type of construction, structure, utilities, square footage, etc. Lenders generally obtain this information from the appraisal re-port. Borrowers seeking a letter of preapproval can provide exam-ple real estate listings of homes where they want to buy. Mortgage programs are structured by the following criteria:

- Maximum loan-to-value (determines minimum down pay-ment)

- Loan purpose (purchase, refinance, cash-out refinance)

- Occupancy (primary residence, 2nd home, investment)

- Property type (1-family detached, 2-4 units, condo, etc.)

Program eligibility, loan pricing, credit score requirements, DTI ratios, payment reserves, and other factors are ascertained based on the above criteria. If the property being purchased is under con-struction, the lender may issue an approval letter that is "subject to completion" of certain steps, and official certificate of occupancy from the city or town.

If the property is considered "manufactured housing," home-buyers may have expanded options or lower down payment re-quirements if the property has a Fannie Mae or Freddie Mac "manufactured housing label."

There is a slight difference among options and underwriting rules within the general category of manufactured homes. "Modu-lar homes," are built in a climate-controlled facility, delivered to the site in 3 or 4 sections and are assembled by a construction crew. Modular homes look like traditional homes due to the wide range of architectural options, and generally eligible for the same loan options as a traditional home, also known as a "stick-built" house.

"Mobile homes,' are eligible for mortgage financing depending upon whether the land is owned or leased, and whether the foun-dation is permanent or non-permanent. Other requirements must be met, such as utilities or minimum square footage. FHA offers many financing options for mobile homes.

Factor #2 - Cash Assets

The second factor is for lenders to determine the borrower(s) have sufficient cash to cover the down payment, closing costs, and any required payment reserves. All funds must be from "acceptable and verifiable" sources. As an example, a non-acceptable source of funds would be the proceeds of an unsecured loan, or cash advance from a revolving credit card. Non-verifiable funds are sources which cannot be validated in writing.

As a rule, mortgage lenders will request photocopies of the most recent two or three months' checking and/or savings accounts. Lenders may verify bank records electronically or employ third-party companies to complete verification steps. For home pur-chases, borrowers must provide a photocopy of the cancelled check given to the seller or realtor as an "earnest money deposit," or provide other records if a check was not used.

When borrowers receive a cash gift from a relative or other associate, the lender needs three items: 1) a letter signed by the donor stating the gift does not have to be repaid; 2) a copy of the donor's financial account where gift funds are held; and 3) evidence the gift was deposited into the borrower(s)' checking account.

Quite often, gift donors question why they must provide copies of their personal bank statement. It is helpful to provide reassurance that "steps and procedures are based on mortgage industry standards and apply uniformly to all borrowers." All funds must be verified, and from all sources.

If a housing agency, nonprofit, or other third party is providing funds to cover all or part of the down payment and/or closing costs, the entity must provide a copy of the agreement. Housing finance agencies typically send agreements directly to the lender.

Most mortgage programs require "payment reserves," requiring new homeowners to have a nest egg to cover initial mortgage payments. Depending upon the loan program and transaction characteristics, reserves must cover the first two months' payments, and can be as many as six months. Acceptable sources of reserve funds include checking, savings, stocks, bonds, mutual funds, certificate of deposits, money market funds, trust accounts, and any vested amount in retirement savings or life insurance policy.

Factor #3 - Income

Mortgage approval is based on the "gross monthly income" of all borrowers named on the loan application. Gross income consists of wages paid before federal or state income tax withholding, and other payroll deductions such as contributions to retirement accounts, health insurance, union dues, etc. The standard mortgage application, known as Form #1003, requires wages to be listed as a monthly figure.

Table 21 can be used to convert various payroll schedules to monthly. For example, people who earn $1,000 weekly might enter $4,000 per month on a loan application. However, their annual income is $52,000, not $48,000. The correct monthly amount is $4,333.

TABLE 21 - MONTHLY INCOME CONVERTER	
Hourly	Multiply the hourly rate of pay by the average number of hours worked each week (or bi-weekly). Multiply the sum by 52 (26 for bi-weekly) to obtain the annual amount. To convert to monthly, divide the annual figure by 12.
Weekly	Multiply one week's base pay by 52 to obtain annual wages. Divide the annual figure by 12.
Bi-weekly	Multiply bi-weekly base pay by 26 to obtain annual wages. Divide by 12.
Semi-monthly	If paid twice per month (such as 1st & 15th), multiply wages by 24, then divide by 12.
Monthly	Enter the monthly gross pay.
Academic Year	If paid over 9 or 10 months, for example, divide the total annual income shown on W-2 form by 12.
Annual	Divide by 12.
Overtime, Bonus or Commissions	The loan application collects separate figures for base pay, overtime, bonus, and commissions. After following the above steps to compute monthly wages, repeat steps separately for overtime, bonus, or commission income.

Conforming loan programs require two year's W-2 forms, a year-to-date paystub, and the last end-of-year paystub. Overtime, commissions, or bonus income is averaged over the past 12 to 18 months—and employers must confirm the additional wages are "likely to continue" in the future.

Child support income is verified with cancelled checks from the payor, and lenders may request a copy of a legal separation agreement that indicates the length of time payments will continue. Alimony or separate maintenance income can be verified through tax returns and/or copies of agreements. As a general rule, non-salaried individuals are asked to provide two years' tax returns to verify income from independent contracting, household workers, tips, and other earned income. Tax returns are required to verify income from interest, dividends, pensions, annuities, and foreign income. Table 22 lists the standard documentation that is required for conforming loans.

TABLE 22 - SELF-EMPLOYED INCOME DOCUMENTS	
Self-Employed 5 Years or more	Two years' Federal 1040 Tax Returns.
Self-Employed 2 to 4 years	Two years' Federal 1040 (plus applicable schedule) • Schedule C or C-EZ (Sole Proprietorship) • Schedule F (Farm) • Schedule E (Rent, Royalty, Partnership, S Corp.) • 1120 Corporation business tax return • 1120 S Corporation business tax return • 1065 Partnership return
Self-Employed Less than 2 years	Two year's Federal 1040 Tax Returns, plus applicable business schedules since business started. W-2 forms from previous employment.
Independent Contractor	Two year's Federal 1040 Tax Returns, plus copies of 1099 forms received from clients or administrator.
Seasonal or Variable Income	Two years' Federal 1040 Tax Returns, plus any W-2s or wage statements sponsor or trade worker's union.

Borrowers who own 25% or more of a business must provide copies of two years' Federal 1040 tax return. Lenders may also request a year-to-date profit and loss statement. In reviewing tax returns and business schedules, mortgage underwriters will make adjustments through a process known as "addbacks." Expenses that are not paid out of pocket, such as depreciation, are added back—essentially increasing net income, which helps borrowers.

Other Sources of Income

Mortgage lenders may consider certain types of income from various sources. Monthly amounts are listed as "other income" on the loan application form. The list below outlines a number of the most common sources, along with a brief summary of eligibility standards for conventional conforming and government-insured mortgages.

Accessory Unit Rental Income

Rental income from an accessory unit dwelling (AUD) may be considered qualifying income. The AUD must be a separate living area that contains a fully functioning kitchen and bathroom. Living areas that are over a garage or in a basement are acceptable if property and zoning conditions are met. Only one accessory unit is permitted, and the unit must have a unique address and be covered by the homeowner's hazard insurance. A property appraiser must provide a comparable sale from a similar property. Any rent added to qualifying income will be the gross rent minus 25% to cover vacancies and other expenses.

Boarder Income

Rental income from boarders may be used to increase qualifying income on principal-residence, single-family homes. The rent paid by the boarder can be any amount; however, the amount that added to the borrower's qualifying income cannot exceed 30% of the borrower's total gross monthly income. Borrowers must submit supporting documentation which verifies a 12-month history of shared residency with the boarder and proof of rental receipts.

Boarder Income for Disabled Borrowers

Borrowers with disabilities can include rental income received from a live-in personal assistant or health aide, including services provided by relatives. Medicaid waiver funds that include room and board are acceptable. Borrowers may be asked to document a 12-

month history of shared residency and rent receipts. Rent to be included cannot exceed 30% of the borrower's total qualifying income.

Disability Income

Borrowers can provide copies of award letters, benefits statements, or a disability policy from the provider. Income must be verified on deposits shown on two recent bank statements. Long-term disability income may be from sources including Social Security, Veterans Administration, workers' compensation, or private disability insurance. Income must be likely to continue for three years, and non-taxable income can be grossed-up by 25%.

Extended Household Income

Income from non-borrowing occupants in a shared household living arrangement may be considered qualifying income. The occupant must verify in writing that they will be living in the home for at least 12 months and provide proof of income. Money received from the extended household member can potentially allow an expanded debt-to-income ratio for the borrower/homeowner.

Food Stamps

For certain mortgage programs, the dollar value of food stamps can be added to qualifying income. Borrowers must provide supporting documentation to verify continuity. Non-taxable income for food stamps, such as the SNAP program, may be grossed-up by 25%.

Foreign Sources

Income from foreign sources may consist of employment income, self-employment, or non-employment types of income. Borrowers must provide copies of recent U.S. federal tax returns along with documentation from the foreign source. Supporting documents must show a history of receipts for the past 12 months and state the likelihood of continuance.

Foster Care

Borrowers who receive income for providing temporary care for one or more children are eligible to use the income for loan qualification. Borrowers must have a two-year history of providing foster care services through a state- or county-sponsored organization. Verification must be provided by the current administrative organization. The amount that may be added to qualifying income cannot exceed 30% of the borrower(s)' total gross income.

Military Income

In addition to base pay, qualifying income for military personnel may include flight or hazard pay, rations, clothing allowance, quarters' allowance, or proficiency pay. Service members and reservists must provide supporting documentation.

Non-occupant Borrower

Income received from a non-occupant borrower may be added to qualifying income for principal residence properties. Non-occupant borrowers must sign the note, mortgage or deed of trust and share liability for the loan. Debt ratios may be expanded, and supporting documentation is required for both the occupant and non-occupant borrowers. Non-occupants cannot have an interest in the real estate transaction, such as the property seller, builder, or real estate broker.

Non-taxable Income

Income that is not subject to taxes may be grossed-up by 25%. Eligible sources include Social Security benefits, workers' compensation, public assistance, food stamps, child support, military benefits, retirement benefits, and other non-taxable sources.

Parsonage Housing Allowance

Income received as an allowance for housing from a parsonage can be added to qualifying income if it will continue for three years. The borrower must provide letters stating the amount of the allowance, the terms under which it is paid, and receipts for the past 12 months.

Public Assistance

Borrowers can include income from public assistance with a letter from the administrative agency stating the amount, frequency, and duration of benefits. Documents must verify that the income is likely to continue for three years. Non-taxable public assistance income can be grossed up by 25% if income is not subject to federal tax.

Retirement Income

Retirement and pension income may be used for qualifying income as long as the income is expected to continue for three years. Borrowers should provide award letters or statements from distributing organizations which state the amount, frequency, and duration of benefits. Income from 401(k) accounts, IRAs, or Keough retirement accounts are acceptable sources of qualifying income as long as the borrower has unrestricted access to accounts, is not subject to penalties, and funds can sufficiently provide distributions for three years. Non-taxable pension or retirement income can be grossed-up by 25% if supporting documentation indicates the income is not subject to federal income tax.

Factor#4 - Credit and Debts

Loan qualification is based on the current credit score and credit history of all borrowers on the loan application. Minimum credit score requirements are established for individual loan programs and CLTV%. There are two main types of monthly debts for loan qualification—fixed-payment and revolving credit. Monthly payments for any fixed-payment debt, such as a car loan, is included if there are ten or more remaining payments. Some programs have a 12-month rule. Borrowers can pay down a loan so that remaining payments are not included in the debt ratio, if they have extra cash.

Student loans are included as a debt, depending upon the status. For loans in deferment or on an income-driven plan, payment is based on the loan servicer's billing statement—even if it is zero. For loans in forbearance, lenders may calculate a payment equal to one percent of the outstanding balance ($100 monthly on a $10,000 balance).

Automobile loans that are reimbursed by an employer are included as a debt, however, the reimbursement amount is added to monthly income. Borrowers who are co-signers on a loan or lease can have the payment excluded if documentation is provided to verify the other party has been making the payments for the past year.

Credit cards from department stores, VISA, Master Card, Discover, etc. are classified as "revolving debt." For loan qualification, lenders will compute a monthly payment of 5% of credit card balances. Balances owed are based on the credit report. Recent payments may not be reflected, and borrowers can submit a copy of a credit card statement to their lender indicating a lower amount.

A co-signed loan is likely to appear on a borrower's credit report. If they can obtain proof that the responsible party has been making timely loan payments for an extended period of time, the lender may remove the debt from qualifying figures.

As explained in Chapter 6, alternative credit documents are acceptable for borrowers with minimal credit history or no credit score. Table 23 lists the types of documentation that can be submitted; however, certain adjustments may be made by the lender.

TABLE 23 - NON-TRADITIONAL CREDIT	
Type	Supporting Documents
Rent	Cash receipts, cancelled checks, reference letter. Document past 12–24 months.
Utilities	Payment history from utility website, bank statements, credit card payments, cash or money order receipts. Document past 6–12 months.
Telephone	Land and/or mobile phones: *same as above*
Insurance	Health or medical, life insurance, auto, boat, vehicle, accident or liability. Obtain recent policy or statement indicating dollar amount paid.
Child Care	Provide past 6–12 months' payment records. Ask provider for a letter to explain other payment terms.
School Tuition	Same as above
Department Stores	Payment history from retailer's website or other payment records for past 6–12 months.
Medical	Letter of explanation from borrower, copies of bills and payment history for applicable time period.
Memberships	Gym memberships, social clubs. Show 6–12 month payment history or obtain statement from facility.
Workers Union	Document payroll deposits, year-to-date and year-end paystubs, and/or letter from union administrator.
Vehicles & Travel	Obtain receipts for car rentals or vehicle loans not reported on credit report. Provide 6 months receipts for ride services, taxi services, or other transportation.
Equipment Lease	Provide lease agreement and payment terms for trade, farm, or fishing equipment and work tools.
Private Loans	Obtain reference letter and show payment history through bank records or cash receipts.

Qualifying Ratios

The debt-to-income (DTI) ratio is the relative difference between the total monthly recurring debt payments and gross monthly income. Permissible DTI ratios can range from 36 to 45. The housing payment ratio is the relative difference between the projected mortgage payment (PITI) and gross monthly income. Permissible housing payment ratios can range from 28% to 33%. Two worksheets are provided below for completing ratios. Shown on the following page in Table 25 is a documents checklist.

TABLE 23 - HOW TO COMPUTE THE DTI RATIO			
Loan Payments	Total of monthly loan payments →	$	
Credit Cards	.05% of all total balance owed →	$	
Housing Payment	Estimated PITI amount →	$	
TOTAL DEBTS	Total of above items →	$	(A)
INCOME	Gross Monthly Income →	$	(B)
DTI Ratio	Divide total debt (A) by income (B)		%

TABLE 24 - HOW TO COMPUTE THE HOUSING PAYMENT RATIO AND DEBT-TO-INCOME RATIO			
Loan Payments	Total of monthly loan payments →	$	
Credit Cards	.05% of all total balance owed →	$	
Housing Payment	Estimated PITI amount →	$	(A)
TOTAL DEBTS	Total of above items →	$	(B)
INCOME	Gross Monthly Income →	$	(C)
Payment Ratio	Divide payment (A) by income (C)		%
DTI Ratio	Divide total debt (B) by income (C)		%

TABLE 25 - DOCUMENT CHECKLIST	
PROPERTY	❐ Sales Contract, signed by all parties
	If applicable to the property, a lender may request: Condominium documents; renovation contract; applicable certificates for energy rating, modular home, or manufactured housing.
CASH ASSETS	❐ Copies of past 3 months' checking account statements ❐ Copies of savings account or any financial statements where funds are used for down payment, closing costs, or payment reserves.
	❐ Copy of cancelled earnest money deposit check ❐ Copy of bank statement showing transaction record
	If applicable, the following items are provided prior to approval:
	❐ Gift letter from donor, and donor source of funds ❐ Asset value statement, if personal item will be sold ❐ Other financial accounts (for payment reserves) ❐ Grant agreement* ❐ Subordinate financing information* **If lender is a housing agency partner, they will have these items*
INCOME all employed borrowers	❐ W-2 tax forms, past two years ❐ Last year's final paystub ❐ Year-to-date paystub
Self-Employed Borrower	❐ Federal 1040 tax return, past two years ❐ Business schedule (Sole-proprietor or Farm) ❐ Business return (Corporation or Partnership) *If self-employed 2 years or less, also provide previous employment documents; if self-employed 5 years or more, business returns may not be required; your lender may request a letter from a CPA (Certified Public Accountant) and/or year-to-date financial statement.*
Other Employment	❐ W-2 forms, past two years *Depending upon type of employment, lender may request two years' federal 1040 tax returns or Worker's Union letter.*
Other Income Sources	*Lender will provide specific document requests based on the type listed on the application, such as child support, disability, retirement, etc.*
CREDIT	*Lender will request items, as needed. Applicants may be asked to write letter to explain credit report errors, omissions, or delinquent payment history. Provide proof of any delinquent bill that was paid.*

CHAPTER 10

Cash-Saving Opportunities

FIVE THOUSAND DOLLARS IN DOWN PAYMENT OR CLOS-ING COST assistance and free homeownership education is available to creditworthy first-time homebuyers with Fannie Mae's Home Ready® First mortgage. In addition to $5,000 in assistance, qualifying homebuyers may also receive the following benefits:

- $500 appraisal reimbursement

- One-year home warranty reimbursement.

- Up to $1,000 title insurance credit when purchasing a Fannie Mae real estate owned (REO) property.

To qualify, borrowers must be a first-time homebuyer and currently reside within certain census tracts in eligible metropolitan statistical areas (MSAs). Homebuyers do not have to purchase a home within the census tract or MSA where they currently reside.

The Fannie Mae Home Ready® First program allows for flexible income limits and acceptance of non-traditional credit history. There are no restrictions on where homebuyers purchase their homes. Borrowers have free access to Fannie's homeownership course, Home View.® Applications can be submitted through a lender that is authorized to sell loans to Fannie Mae, including state-chartered housing finance agencies.[106]

Fannie Mae Home Ready® First

Eligible MSAs (where homebuyer currently resides)

Borrowers must reside in an <u>eligible census tract</u> within the MSAs listed.[107] The mortgage lender will have access to the census tract information.

- Atlanta-Sandy Springs-Alpharetta, GA
- Baltimore-Columbia-Towson, MD
- Brownsville-Harlingen, TX
- Chicago-Naperville-Elgin, IL-IN
- Cleveland-Elyria, OH
- Dallas-Fort Worth-Arlington, TX
- Detroit-Warren-Dearborn, MI
- Houston-The Woodlands-Sugar Land, TX
- McAllen-Edinburg-Mission, TX
- Memphis, TN-MS-AR
- Miami-Fort Lauderdale-Pompano Beach, FL
- New York-Newark-Jersey City, NY-NJ-PA
- Oklahoma City, OK
- Orlando-Kissimmee-Sanford, FL
- Philadelphia-Camden-Wilmington, PA-NJ-DE-MD
- Phoenix-Mesa-Chandler, AZ
- Riverside-San Bernardino-Ontario, CA
- San Antonio-New Braunfels, TX
- St. Louis, MO-IL
- Tampa-St. Petersburg-Clearwater, FL
- Washington-Arlington-Alexandria, DC-VA-MD

Fannie Mae Home Ready®

$ 2,500 in down payment assistance

Fannie Mae's Home Ready® loan program offers expanded financing flexibilities and low down payment requirements. The program is available to both first-time and repeat homebuyers. With this program, $2,500 is available to very low-income purchase (VLIP) borrowers. Key features are summarized:

- Borrowers with a qualifying income of less than or equal to 50% of the applicable area median income (AMI) of the subject property location are eligible.

- The full amount of the $2,500 must be provided directly to the borrower through the transaction, such as being applied to down payment and closing costs, including escrows and mortgage insurance premiums.

- Low down payment of 3%. Financing up to 97% LTV% on purchase and refinance transactions.

- Flexible source of funds can be used for down payment and closing costs, with no minimum contribution required from the borrower's own funds for 1-unit homes.

- Gifts, grants from lenders or other eligible entities, and subordinate financing from housing finance agencies that meet Fannie Mae's Community Seconds® requirements.

- Innovative underwriting flexibilities include rental unit and boarder income, and non-occupant borrowers, such as parents.

Freddie Mac Home Possible®

$ 2,500 in down payment assistance

Freddie Mac's Home Possible® loan program offers $2,500 credit to assist with down payment and other costs at closing to potential homebuyers earning 50% of area median income (AMI). The program is available to very low-income purchase (VLIP) borrowers.

Listed below are the general features of Freddie Mac's Home Possible® mortgage programs:

- Available to low-income borrowers (up to 80% of AMI) and very-low income borrowers (up to. 50% of AMI).

- Borrowers can have additional financed properties.

- Non-occupant co-borrowers may help borrowers qualify for a 1-unit property.

- Many types of down payment sources are acceptable, including family, employer-assistance programs, secondary financing, and sweat equity.

- At 20 percent equity, borrowers may cancel mortgage insurance.

- Credit flexibilities.

Freddie Mac Home One®

Available to qualified first-time homebuyers for a low down payment of just 3%, the Freddie Mac Home One® mortgage is a down payment option that serves the needs of many first-time homebuyers, along with no cash-out refinance borrowers. Listed are key features of the program:

- 3% down payment

- No income limits

- No borrower geographic limits

- New purchases only

- 1-unit homes

- All borrowers must occupy as primary residence

- At least one borrower must be a first-time homebuyer

- Cash-out refinance on existing Freddie Mac owned mortgages

- Allows both Affordable Seconds® and other secondary financing

- Accommodates various property types

- Homeownership education required when all borrowers are first-time homebuyers

Private Mortgage Insurance

Private Mortgage Insurance (PMI) is required for any conventional mortgage that has a loan-to-value ratio over 80%. This rule applies to all conventional mortgages, including non-conforming and jumbo mortgages. Private mortgage insurance is also required for refinance transactions, where the final LTV% is determined by the property appraisal.

The cost of private mortgage insurance is structured according to the loan-to-value percent, and borrowers typically pay an "up-front premium" plus a monthly premium. However, there are many options available, which may be referred to "single-premium," or "split-premium" coverage. Another factor related to the cost of PMI is the "level of coverage" that is required for the specific mortgage program. The coverage level changes according to LTV% and other loan characteristics.

TABLE 26 PRIVATE MORTGAGE INSURANCE		
CLTV%	Loan Amount	Monthly Premium
90%	$ 100,000	$ 30
	$ 200,000	$ 55
	$ 300,000	$ 75
95%	$ 100,000	$ 45
	$ 200,000	$ 80
	$ 300,000	$ 115
Figures are estimated, and based on 7.00% interest, 30-year fixed rate mortgage.		

The monthly premium cost is structured according to the loan-to-value %. The lower the LTV%, the lower the monthly cost.

PMI Cancellation

The "Homeowners Protection Act" took effect in July 1999, and is also known as the PMI Cancellation Act. The Act established provisions for consumers to cancel their private mortgage insurance when the loan-to-value reaches 80% of the "original value." Properties must be the borrower's primary residence, and the law applies to all residential property types, including mobile homes. Borrowers may initiate cancelation or it may automatically be terminated by the loan servicer.[108]

CHAPTER 11

Housing Finance Agencies

EVERY STATE IN AMERICA HAS A STATE-CHARTERED HOUS-ING AGENCY that helps residents of the state finance their home. Known as HFAs, entities are independent organizations that operate under the direction of a board of directors appointed by the state governor.

HFAs fund and administer lower-interest rate loans that are originated by local banks, thrifts, credit unions, and mortgage companies. HFAs offer both conventional and government-insured mortgages, and they sell loans to Fannie Mae and Freddie Mac. Each state housing agency creates mortgage programs that align with state population characteristics, housing costs, and median household income.

As a general rule, borrowers must meet certain eligibility rules regarding maximum income and maximum purchase price (or loan amount). Rules are established on a per-program basis, such as first-time homebuyer mortgages, renovation loans, down payment assistance and so forth. There are usually a number of programs that have no borrower income restrictions. Special incentives are often available for homes purchased in a high-needs area, or certain city, town, or county.

Nearly all state-charted housing finance agencies throughout the country offer homebuyer assistance, including second mortgages that may be used to cover the down payment and closing costs. Subordinate lien programs are often zero- or very-low interest, and structured as soft seconds, deferred payment loans, and forgivable loans.

For the most part, borrowers can submit an application directly to the housing agency, however, every HPA works in collaboration with local lenders. On the HPA website, homebuyers can search for a list of approved local lenders. It's worthwhile to view the various programs—as well as interest rates, points, and fees that are being offered by the agency. HPAs generally offer tax credit certificates, which are bottom-line, dollar-for-dollar tax credits to homebuyers.

First generation homebuyer programs, including the national Down payment fund explained earlier in Chapter 7, are available from most housing partnership agencies.

A complete listing of state housing finance agencies are shown on the following pages.

State Directory of Housing Finance Agencies

Alabama Housing Finance Agency

7460 Halcyon Pointe Drive, Suite 200

Montgomery AL 36117

www.ahfa.com

Alaska Housing Finance Agency

4300 Boniface Parkway
Anchorage AK 99504
www.ahfc.us

Arizona Department of Housing

1110 W. Washington #280
Phoenix AZ 85007
www.housing.az.gov

Arkansas Development Finance Agency

900 West Capitol, Suite 310
Little Rock AR 72201
www.adfa.arkansas.gov

California Housing Finance Agency

500 Capitol Mall, Ste. 1400
Sacramento CA 95814
www.calhfa.ca.gov

100 Corporate Pointe, Ste. 250
Culver City, CA 90230

Connecticut Housing Finance Authority

999 West Street

Rocky Hill CT 06067

www.chfa.org

District of Columbia Housing Finance Agency

815 Florida Avenue, NW

Washington, D.C. 20001

www.dchfa.org

Florida Housing Finance Corporation

227 N. Bronough Street, Suite 5000

Tallahassee, Florida 32301

www.floridahousing.org

Georgia Department of Community Affairs

60 Executive Park South, NE

Atlanta GA 30329

www.dca.ga.gov

Hawaii Housing & Finance Development

677 Queen Street

Honolulu, Hawaii 96813

www.dbedt.hawaii.gov/hhfdc

Idaho Housing and Finance Agency

506 S Woodruff Ave

Idaho Falls, ID 83401

www.idahohousing.com

Illinois Housing Development Authority

111 E. Wacker Drive, Suite 1000
Chicago, IL 60601
www.ihda.org

Indiana Housing & Community Development

30 South Meridian Street, Suite 1000
Indianapolis IN 46204)
www.in.gov/ihcda

Iowa Finance Agency

2015 Grand Ave.
Des Moines, Iowa 50312
www.iowafinanceauthority.gov

Kansas Housing Resources Corporation

611 S. Kansas Avenue, Suite 300
Topeka KS 66603
www.kshousingcorp.org

Kentucky Housing Corporation

1231 Louisville Road
Frankfort, Kentucky 40601
www.kyhousing.org

Louisiana Housing Corporation

2415 Quail Drive
Baton Rouge, LA 70808
www.lhc.la.gov

Maine State Housing Agency

353 Water Street

Augusta ME 04330

www.mainehousing.org

Maryland Dept. of Housing & Community Development

Maryland Mortgage Program

7800 Harkins Road, Lanham MD 20706

mmp.maryland.gov

Massachusetts Housing Finance Agency

One Beacon Street

Boston, MA 02108

www.masshousing.com

Michigan State Housing Development Authority

735 Michigan Avenue

Lansing MI 48909

www.michigan.gov/mshda

Cadillac Place, 3028 W. Grand Blvd., Suite 4-600

Detroit MI 48202

Minnesota Housing Finance Agency

400 Sibley Street, Suite 300

Saint Paul MN 55101

www.mnhousing.gov

Mississippi Home Corporation

735 Riverside Dr.
Jackson MS 39202
www.mshomecorp.com

Missouri Housing Development Corporation

920 Main Street, Suite 1400
Kansas City MO 64105
www.mhdc.com

505 N. 7th Street, 20th Floor, Ste 2000
St. Louis MO 63101

Montana Dept. of Commerce

Housing Division
301 S. Park Ave, Ste. 240
Helena MT 59620
www.housing.mt.gov

Nebraska Investment Finance Authority

200 Commerce Court, 1230 O Street
Lincoln NE 68508
www.nifa.org

Nevada Housing Division

Dept. of Business & Industry
3300 W Sahara Ave, Ste. 300
Las Vegas NV 89102
www.housing.nv.gov

1830 College Parkway Ste. 200
Carson City, NV 89706

New Hampshire Housing Finance Authority

PO Box 5087

Manchester NH 03108

www.gonewhampshirehousing.com

New Jersey Housing & Mortgage Finance Agency

637 South Clinton Avenue

Trenton, NJ 08611

www.state.nj.us/dca/hmfa

New Mexico Mortgage Finance Agency

344 4th Street SW

Albuquerque NM 87102

www.housingnm.org

New York State Homes and Community Renewal

State of New York Mortgage Agency (SONYMA)

641 Lexington Ave # 4

New York, NY 10022

www.nyshcr.org/SONYMA

North Carolina Housing Finance Agency

3508 Bush Street

Raleigh NC 27608

www.nchfa.com

North Dakota Housing Finance Agency

2624 Vermont Avenue

Bismarck ND 58502

www.ndhfa.org

The Ohio Housing Finance Agency

57 E. Main St.
Columbus OH 43215
www.myohiohome.org

Oklahoma Housing Finance Agency

100 NW 63rd Street, Ste. 200
Oklahoma City OK 73116
www.ok.gov/ohfa

Oregon Housing and Community Services

725 Summer St NE, Ste B
Salem, OR 97301
www.oregon.gov/ohcs

Pennsylvania Housing Finance Agency

211 North Front St.
Harrisburg PA 17101
www.phfa.org

2275 Swallow Hill Rd, Suite 200
Pittsburgh PA 15220

104 West Main St, Suite 3
Norristown PA 19401

Rhode Island Housing

44 Washington Street
Providence, RI 02903
www.rhodeislandhousing.org

South Carolina State Housing Finance & Development

300 Outlet Pointe Blvd C

Columbia, SC 29210

www.schousing.com

South Dakota Housing Development Agency

3060 East Elizabeth Street

Pierre SD 57501

www.sdhda.org

Tennessee Housing Development Agency

Andrew Jackson Building, Third Floor

502 Deaderick St.

Nashville TN 37243

www.thda.org

Texas Dept. of Housing and Community Affairs

221 East 11th Street

Austin, Texas 78701

www.tdhca.state.tx.us

Utah Housing Corporation

2479 South Lake Park Blvd.

West Valley City, Utah 84120

www.utahhousingcorp.org

Vermont Housing Finance Agency

164 Saint Paul Street

Burlington, VT 05402

www.vhfa.org

Virginia Housing Development Agency

601 S. Belvidere Street
Richmond VA 23220
www.vhda.com

Virginia Housing Center
4224 Cox Road, Glen Allen VA 23060

Southwest Virginia Housing Center
E. Main Street & Church St., Wytheville VA 24382

Washington State Housing Finance Commission

1000 Second Avenue, Suite 2700
Seattle WA 98104
www.wshfc.org

West Virginia Housing Development Fund

5710 MacCorkle Avenue SE
Charleston WV 25304
www.wvhdf.com

Wisconsin Housing & Economic Development

201 W. Washington Ave., Suite 700
Madison WI 53703
611 W. National Avenue, Suite 110
Milwaukee WI 53204
www.wheda.com

Wyoming Community Development Authority

155 N. Beech Street
Casper WY 82602
www.wyomingcda.com

CHAPTER 12

Qualified Mortgage Ability-to-Repay Rule

THE 2010 DODD-FRANK QUALIFIED MORTGAGE AND ABIL-ITY-TO-REPAY rule was adopted by Congress for virtually all closed-end residential mortgages loans. The Qualified Mortgage (QM) Rule was part of the Wall Street Reform and Consumer Protection Act, known as the Dodd-Frank Act.[109] QM loans prohibit risky loan features such as an interest-only loan period, where no principal is paid; negative amortization, which allows loan principal to increase over time; balloon payments, or other surprise features; and loan terms longer than 30 years.

QM rules place specific limits on loan pricing. The annual percentage rate (APR) on a QM loan cannot be higher than a certain threshold, which varies based on the type or size of the mortgage. The threshold is based on the Average Prime Offer Rate (APOR), which is derived from average interest rates, points, and other loan pricing terms currently offered to consumers by a representative sample of creditors for mortgage loans that have low-risk pricing characteristics.

With a QM mortgage, there can be no excess upfront points and fees. There are limits on the amount of certain up-front points and fees a lender can charge, depending upon the size of the loan. Certain charges such as FHA insurance are premiums, for example, are not included in this limit. If the points and fees exceed a certain threshold, then the loan cannot be considered a Qualified Mortgage.

For a loan to be a Qualified Mortgage, the lender must consider and verify the borrower(s)' current monthly income, assets, and monthly debt. The lender must also consider either how much income can go towards the monthly debt, including the mortgage payment and all other monthly debt payments, known as the debt-to-income ratio or DTI. The QM rule also considers how much of income is left over after paying all monthly debts, known as residual income.

Qualified Mortgage / Ability-to-Repay Requirements

The Consumer Financial Protection Bureau (CFPB) adopted a rule in January 2013 that implemented the Dodd Frank's Ability-to-Repay and Qualified Mortgage provisions, referred to as the QTR/QM Rule.[110] The ATR/QM Rule requires a creditor to make a reasonable and good-faith determination of a consumer's ability to repay at or before consummation of a QM loan. To satisfy the rule's general ATR standard, a creditor must consider eight factors:

1. The consumer's current or reasonably expected income or assets (other than the value of the dwelling and attached real property securing the loan);

2. The consumer's employment status, if the credit relies upon income from employment in determining the ATR;

3. The consumer's monthly mortgage loan payment;

4. The consumer's monthly payment for mortgage-related obligations (*e.g.*, property taxes, homeowner's association and condominium fees, and certain ongoing expenses that are related to the mortgage loan and required by the creditor);

5. The consumer's monthly payments on simultaneous loans that are secured by the same property;

6. The consumer's current debt obligations, alimony, and child-support payments;

7. The consumer's monthly debt-to-income ratio or residual income;

8. The consumer's credit history.

The ATR/QM Rule does not ban any particular loan features or transaction types, but a particular loan to a particular consumer is not permissible if the creditor does not make a reasonable, good-faith determination that the consumer has the ability to repay. For example, it is no longer possible to originate loans based on stated income. Additionally, the Rule has specific requirements and limitations related to loans with certain nontraditional features.

The creditor must also verify information it relied on when making its ATR determination. The ATR/QM Rule provides a presumption that a creditor has complied with the ATR requirement if the creditor originates a QM. In exchange for meeting certain requirements, QMs receive either a conclusive or a rebuttable presumption that the creditor complied with the ATR/QM Rule's requirements.

Except for Seasoned QMs, the type of presumption depends on the pricing of the loan, *i.e.*, whether the loan is not higher-priced or is higher-priced. A creditor is not required to comply with the Rule's ATR requirements if the creditor satisfies the Rule's conditions for the refinancing of a non-standard mortgage loan to a standard mortgage loan. The ATR/QM rule implements other provisions of the Dodd-Frank Act that limit prepayment penalties.[111]

Applicable Transactions

The ATR/QM Rule applies to almost all closed end mortgage transactions, including any real property attached to the dwelling. This means that the Rule generally applies to loans made to consumers and secured by residential structures that contain one to four units, including condominiums and co-ops. The ATR/QM Rule is not limited to first-lien loans or to loans secured by a primary residence. Specifically, ATR requirements do not apply to any of the following: open-end credit plans; timeshare plans; reverse mortgages; temporary or bridge loans; construction phase of 12 months or less; and loans secured by vacant land.

Exemptions

Extensions of credit made by housing finance agencies directly to consumers, as well as extensions of credit made by other creditors pursuant to a program administered by a housing finance agency, are exempt from the ATR requirements. This ATR exemption applies to extensions of credit made pursuant to a program administered by a housing finance agency, regardless of the funding source (e.g. federal, state, or other sources). Certain types of creditors or loan programs may be exempt from the ATR/QM Rule's ATR requirements. Extensions of credit made by any of the following creditors are exempt from the ATR/QM Rule's ATR requirements:

- Creditors designated by the U.S. Department of the Treasury as Community Development Financial Institutions.

- Creditors designated by the Department of Housing and Urban Development (HUD) as either a community housing development organization or a down payment assistance provider of secondary financing, under certain conditions.

- Creditors designated as nonprofit organizations under section 501(c)(3) of the Internal Revenue Code of 1986 that extend dwelling-secured credit no more than 200 times annually, provide dwelling-secured credit only to low-to-moderate income consumers, and follow their own written procedures to determine that consumers have a reasonable ability to repay their loans. Some subordinate liens are not counted towards the 200-credit extension limit.

Extensions of credit made pursuant to an Emergency Economic Stabilization Act program, such as a State Hardest Hit Fund program, are also exempt from the ATR requirements. The exemptions above apply to all loans made by these credits or pursuant to these loan programs, provided the conditions for the exemption are satisfied. An exempt loan remains exempt even if it is sold, assigned, or otherwise transferred to a creditor that would not qualify for the exemption.[112]

Documentation and Verification

Creditors are required to consider and document supplemental information provided by the applicant, whether the documents were requested by the company or not. Creditors must retain all records, worksheets, and supporting documentation used in the analysis of the applicant's ability to repay. The verified income should reasonably demonstrate the applicant's ability to repay the loan.[113] Illustrated are verification methods:

- The ability to repay may be documented through verification of bank deposits, other available assets, or gifts.

- The applicant's start date of employment or relocation may be considered to further reasonably determine ability to repay.

Analysis of Income and Total Obligations

The ATR analysis must determine whether an applicant will have the ability to repay an offered loan based on the applicant's existing income and credit obligations. The institution needs to consider, verify, and document the following criteria:

- The gross income of all applicants, using the underwriting standards for acceptable and verifiable sources of income.

- The fixed expenses of all applicants, using the underwriting standards for fixed monthly debt, including minimum monthly payments for revolving credit. Fixed expenses may include child support, alimony payments, separate maintenance, condominium or housing association dues, property taxes and hazard insurance, and whether taxes and hazard insurance are to be escrowed.

In accordance with ECOA, the applicant only needs to list sources of income that will be relied upon to repay the loan. Appendix Q to Part 1026 of the Dodd-Frank amendment provides the standards for determining monthly debt and income for the calculation of debt-to-income ratio to determine whether a loan meets QM standards.[114]

Prohibited Activities

During the application interview, processing, or approval of the loan, employees of the creditor may not do the following:

- Ignore facts or circumstances which would change or affect the applicant(s)' ability to repay.

- Advise or imply to applicants that their income is not relevant to the loan transaction.

- Advise or induce applicants to refinance an existing loan or enter into a new financial obligation without performing the ability-to-repay analysis.

- Base the applicants' ability to pay upon projected equity from the sale or refinancing of the applicant(s)' property.

Balloon Payments

For an originated loan with a balloon payment, the institution may consider the sale or refinance of the applicant's collateral when evaluating an applicant's ability to make the balloon payment. In such cases, the company will consider the due date of the balloon payment if there is a reasonable expectation of sufficient equity in the property through a sale or refinance of the residence.

Negative Changes

If the institution becomes aware of a material negative change during the loan processing steps, the institution will immediately perform another ability-to-repay analysis. For third-party originated loans, the company must send a notice to the applicant disclosing the negative change and state the change may affect the applicant's ability to repay.

CHAPTER 13

Equal Credit Opportunity Act

THE EQUAL CREDIT OPPORTUNITY ACT PROHIBITS DISCRIM-INATION against credit applicants on the basis of race, color, religion, national origin, sex, marital status, age, whether they are a recipient of public assistance, and whether they have exercised their rights under the Consumer Credit Protection Act.[115]

The United States Department of Justice may file a lawsuit under ECOA where there is a pattern or practice of discrimination. In cases involving discrimination in home mortgage loans or home improvement loans, the Department may file suit under both the Fair Housing Act and ECOA.

Individuals who believe that they have been the victims of any unfair credit transaction involving residential property may file a complaint with the Department of Housing and Urban Development (HUD) or may file their own lawsuit.[116]

Other federal agencies have general regulatory authority over certain types of lenders, and they monitor creditors for their compliance with ECOA. ECOA requires these agencies to refer matters to the Justice Department when there is reason to believe that a creditor is engaged in a pattern or practice of discrimination which violates ECOA.[117]

Subject matter included in this chapter covers key rules pertaining to credit applications for residential real estate transactions.

§ 202.4 General Rules

Discouragement

A creditor shall not make any oral or written statement, in advertising or otherwise, to applicants or prospective applicants that would discourage on a prohibited basis a reasonable person from making or pursuing an application.

Form of disclosures

A creditor that provides in writing any disclosures or information required by this regulation must provide the disclosures in a clear and conspicuous manner and in a form the applicant may retain, except for the disclosures required by the regulation in §202.5 and §202.13. Disclosures required by this part that are required to be given in writing may be provided to the applicant in electronic form, subject to compliance with the consumer consent and other applicable provisions of the Electronic Signatures in Global and National Commerce Act (E-Sign Act).

§ 202.5 Rules Concerning Requests for Information

A creditor may inquire about the race, colour, religion, national origin, or sex of an applicant or any other person in connection with a credit transaction for the purpose of conducting a self-test that meets the requirements of §202.15. A creditor that makes such an inquiry shall disclose orally or in writing, at the time the information is requested, that:

1. The applicant will not be required to provide the information;

2. The creditor is requesting the information to monitor its compliance with the federal Equal Credit Opportunity Act;

3. Federal law prohibits the creditor from discriminating on the basis of this information, or on the basis of an applicant's decision not to furnish the information; and

4. If applicable, certain information will be collected based on visual observation or surname if not provided by the applicant or other person.

Other limitations on information requests

Marital status

If an applicant applies for individual unsecured credit, a creditor shall not inquire about the applicant's marital status unless the applicant resides in a community property state or is relying on property located in such a state as a basis for repayment of the credit requested.

If an application is for other than individual unsecured credit, a creditor may inquire about the applicant's marital status, but shall use only the following terms: *married, unmarried, and separated.* A creditor may explain that the category *unmarried* includes single, divorced, and widowed persons.

Income from alimony, child support, or separate maintenance

A creditor shall not inquire whether income stated in an application is derived from alimony, child support, or separate maintenance payments unless the creditor discloses to the applicant that such income need not be revealed if the applicant does not want the creditor to consider it in determining the applicant's creditworthiness.

Childbearing, childrearing

A creditor shall not inquire about birth control practices, intentions concerning the bearing or rearing of children, or capability to bear children. A creditor may inquire about the number and ages of an applicant's dependents or about dependent-related financial obligations or expenditures, provided such information is requested without regard to sex, marital status, or any other prohibited basis.

§ 202.6 Rules Concerning Evaluation of Applications

General rule concerning use of information

Except as otherwise provided in the Act and this regulation, a creditor may consider any information obtained, so long as the information is not used to discriminate against an applicant on a prohibited basis.

Specific rules concerning use of information

Except as provided in the Act and this regulation, a creditor shall not take a prohibited basis into account in any system of evaluating the creditworthiness of applicants.

Age, Receipt of Public Assistance

Except as permitted in this paragraph, a creditor shall not take into account an applicant's age (provided that the applicant has the capacity to enter into a binding contract) or whether an applicant's income derives from any public assistance program.

i.   In an empirically derived, demonstrably, and statistically sound credit scoring system, a creditor may use an applicant's age as a predictive variable, provided that the age of an elderly applicant is not assigned a negative factor or value.

ii.   In a judgmental system of evaluating creditworthiness, a creditor may consider an applicant's age or whether an applicant's income derives from any public assistance program only for the purpose of determining a pertinent element of creditworthiness.

iii. In any system of evaluating creditworthiness, a creditor may consider the age of an elderly applicant when such age is used to favor the elderly applicant in extending credit.

Childbearing, childrearing

In evaluating creditworthiness, a creditor shall not make assumptions or use aggregate statistics relating to the likelihood that any category of persons will bear or rear children or will, for that reason, receive diminished or interrupted income in the future.

Telephone listing

A creditor shall not take into account whether there is a telephone listing in the name of an applicant for consumer credit but may take into account whether there is a telephone in the applicant's residence.

Income

A creditor shall not discount or exclude from consideration the income of an applicant or the spouse of an applicant because of a prohibited basis or because the income is derived from part-time employment or is an annuity, pension, or other retirement benefit; a creditor may consider the amount and probable continuance of any income in evaluating an applicant's creditworthiness. When an applicant relies on alimony, child support, or separate maintenance payments in applying for credit, the creditor shall consider such payments as income to the extent that they are likely to be consistently made.

Credit history

To the extent that a creditor considers credit history in evaluating the creditworthiness of similarly qualified applicants for a similar type and amount of credit, in evaluating an applicant's creditworthiness a creditor shall consider:

i. The credit history, when available, of accounts designated as accounts that the applicant and the applicant's spouse are permitted to use or for which both are contractually liable;

ii. On the applicant's request, any information the applicant may present that tends to indicate the credit history being considered by the creditor does not accurately reflect the applicant's creditworthiness; and

iii. On the applicant's request, the credit history, when available, of any account reported in the name of the applicant's spouse or former spouse that the applicant can demonstrate accurately reflects the applicant's creditworthiness.

Immigration status

A creditor may consider the applicant's immigration status or status as a permanent resident of the United States, and any additional information that may be necessary to ascertain the creditor's rights and remedies regarding repayment.

Marital status

Except as otherwise permitted or required by law, a creditor shall evaluate married and unmarried applicants by the same standards; and in evaluating joint applicants, a creditor shall not treat applicants differently based on the existence, absence, or likelihood of a marital relationship between the parties.

Race, color, religion, national origin, sex

Except as otherwise permitted or required by law, a creditor shall not consider race, color, religion, national origin, or sex (or an applicant's or other person's decision not to provide the information) in any aspect of a credit transaction.

§ 202.7 Rules Concerning Extensions of Credit

Requiring re-application

A creditor may require a re-application for an open-end account on the basis of a change in the marital status of an applicant who is contractually liable if the credit granted was based in whole or in part on income of the applicant's spouse and if information available to the creditor indicates that the applicant's income may not support the amount of credit currently available.

Signature of spouse or other person

Rule for qualified applicant

Except as provided in this paragraph, a creditor shall not require the signature of an applicant's spouse or other person, other than a joint applicant, on any credit instrument if the applicant qualifies under the creditor's standards of creditworthiness for the amount and terms of the credit requested. A creditor shall not deem the submission of a joint financial statement or other evidence of jointly held assets as an application for joint credit.

Unsecured credit

If an applicant requests unsecured credit and relies in part upon property that the applicant owns jointly with another person to satisfy the creditor's standards of creditworthiness, the creditor may require the signature of the other person only on the instrument(s) necessary, or reasonably believed by the creditor to be necessary, under the law of the state in which the property is located, to enable the creditor to reach the property being relied upon in the event of the death or default of the applicant.

Unsecured credit—community property states

If a married applicant requests unsecured credit and resides in a community property state, or if the applicant is relying on property located in such a state, a creditor may require the signature of the spouse on any instrument necessary, or reasonably believed by the creditor to be necessary, under applicable state law to make the community property available to satisfy the debt in the event of default if:

i.   Applicable state law denies the applicant power to manage or control sufficient community property to qualify for the credit requested under the creditor's standards of creditworthiness; and

ii. The applicant does not have sufficient separate property to qualify for the credit requested without regard to community property.

Secured credit

If an applicant requests secured credit, a creditor may require the signature of the applicant's spouse or other person on any instrument necessary, or reasonably believed by the creditor to be necessary, under applicable state law to make the property being offered as security available to satisfy the debt in the event of default, for example, an instrument to create a valid lien, pass clear title, waive inchoate rights, or assign earnings.

Additional parties

If, under a creditor's standards of creditworthiness, the personal liability of an additional party is necessary to support the credit requested, a creditor may request a co-signer, guarantor, endorser, or similar party. The applicant's spouse may serve as an additional party, but the creditor shall not require that the spouse be the additional party.

Rights of additional parties

A creditor shall not impose requirements upon an additional party that the creditor is prohibited from imposing upon an applicant under this section.

§ 202.8 Special Purpose Credit Programs

Standards for Programs

Subject to the provisions of this section, the Act and this regulation permit a creditor to extend special purpose credit to applicants who meet eligibility requirements under the following types of credit programs:

1) Any credit assistance program expressly authorized by federal or state law for the benefit of an economically disadvantaged class of persons;

2) Any credit assistance program offered by a not-for-profit organization, as defined under section 501(c) of the Internal Revenue Code of 1954, as amended, for the benefit of its members or for the benefit of an economically disadvantaged class of persons; or

3) Any special purpose credit program offered by a for-profit organization, or in which such an organization participates to meet special social needs, if:

   i.   The program is established and administered pursuant to a written plan that identifies the class of persons that the program is designed to benefit and sets forth the procedures and standards for extending credit pursuant to the program; and

   ii. The program is established and administered to extend credit to a class of persons who, under the organization's customary standards of creditworthiness, probably would not receive such credit or would receive it on less favorable terms than are ordinarily available to other applicants applying to the organization for a similar type and amount of credit.

Common Characteristics

A program described in this section qualifies as a special purpose credit program only if it was established and is administered so as not to discriminate against an applicant on any prohibited basis; however, all program participants may be required to share one or more common characteristics (for example, race, national origin, or sex) so long as the program was not established and is not administered with the purpose of evading the requirements of the Act or this regulation.

§ 202.9 Notification

Notification of Action Taken

ECOA Notice, and Statement of Specific Reasons

When notification is required

A creditor shall notify an applicant of action taken within:

i.   30 days after receiving a completed application concerning the creditor's approval of, counteroffer to, or adverse action on the application;

ii.   30 days after taking adverse action on an incomplete application, unless notice is provided in accordance with this section;

iii. 30 days after taking adverse action on an existing account; or

iv.   90 days after notifying the applicant of a counteroffer if the applicant does not expressly accept or use the credit offered.

Content of notification when adverse action is taken

A notification given to an applicant when adverse action is taken shall be in writing and shall contain a statement of the action taken; the name and address of the creditor; a statement of the provisions of §701(a) of the Act; the name and address of the federal agency that administers compliance with respect to the creditor; and either:

i.   A statement of specific reasons for the action taken; or

ii.   A disclosure of the applicant's right to a statement of specific reasons within 30 days if the statement is requested within 60 days of the creditor's notification. The disclosure shall include the name, address, and telephone number of the person or office from which the statement of reasons can be obtained. If the creditor chooses to provide the reasons orally, the creditor shall also disclose the applicant's right to have them confirmed in writing within 30 days of receiving the applicant's written request for confirmation.

Form of ECOA notice and statement of specific reasons

ECOA notice

To satisfy the disclosure requirements of this section regarding section 701(a) of the Act, the creditor shall provide a notice that is substantially similar to the following:

The federal Equal Credit Opportunity Act prohibits creditors from discriminating against credit applicants on the basis of race, color, religion, national origin, sex, marital status, age (provided the applicant has the capacity to enter into a binding contract); because all or part of the applicant's income derives from any public assistance program; or because the applicant has in good faith exercised any right under the Consumer Credit Protection Act. The federal agency that administers compliance with this law concerning this creditor is [name and address as specified by the appropriate agency listed in appendix A of this regulation].

Statement of Specific Reasons

The statement of reasons for adverse action required by this section must be specific and indicate the principal reason(s) for the adverse action. Statements that the adverse action was based on the creditor's internal standards or policies or that the applicant, joint applicant, or similar party failed to achieve a qualifying score on the creditor's credit scoring system are insufficient.

Incomplete applications

Notice alternatives

Within 30 days after receiving an application that is incomplete regarding matters that an applicant can complete, the creditor shall notify the applicant either:

i.   Of action taken, in accordance with this section; or

ii.   Of the incompleteness, in accordance with this section.

Notice of incompleteness

If additional information is needed from an applicant, the creditor shall send a written notice to the applicant specifying the information needed, designating a reasonable period of time for the applicant to provide the information, and informing the applicant that failure to provide the information requested will result in no further consideration being given to the application. The creditor shall have no further obligation under this section if the applicant fails to respond within the designated time period. If the applicant supplies the requested information within the designated time period, the creditor shall take action on the application and notify the applicant in accordance with this section.

Oral request for information

At its option, a creditor may inform the applicant orally of the need for additional information. If the application remains incomplete, the creditor shall send a notice in accordance with this section.

Oral notifications by small-volume creditors

In the case of a creditor that did not receive more than 150 applications during the preceding calendar year, the requirements of this section (including statements of specific reasons) are satisfied by oral notifications.

Withdrawal of approved application

When an applicant submits an application and the parties contemplate that the applicant will inquire about its status, if the creditor approves the application and the applicant has not inquired within 30 days after applying, the creditor may treat the application as withdrawn and need not comply with this section.

Multiple applicants

When an application involves more than one applicant, notification need only be given to one of them but must be given to the primary applicant where one is readily apparent.

Applications submitted through a third party

When an application is made on behalf of an applicant to more than one creditor and the applicant expressly accepts or uses credit offered by one of the creditors, notification of action taken by any of the other creditors is not required. If no credit is offered or if the applicant does not expressly accept or use the credit offered, each creditor taking adverse action must comply with this section, directly or through a third party. A notice given by a third party shall disclose the identity of each creditor on whose behalf the notice is given.

§ 202.14 Rules on Providing Appraisal Reports

Providing appraisals

A creditor shall provide a copy of an appraisal report used in connection with an application for credit that is to be secured by a lien on a dwelling. A creditor shall comply with either of the two options below:

Upon request

A creditor that does not routinely provide appraisal reports shall provide a copy upon an applicant's written request.

Notice

A creditor that provides appraisal reports only upon request shall notify an applicant in writing of the right to receive a copy of an appraisal report. The notice may be given at any time during the application process but no later than when the creditor provides notice of action taken under § 202.9 of this regulation. The notice shall specify that the applicant's request must be in writing, give the creditor's mailing address, and state the time for making the request as provided in this section.

Delivery

A creditor shall mail or deliver a copy of the appraisal report promptly (generally within 30 days) after the creditor receives an applicant's request, receives the report, or receives reimbursement from the applicant for the report, whichever is last to occur. A creditor need not provide a copy when the applicant's request is received more than 90 days after the creditor has provided notice of action taken on the application under § 202.9 of this regulation or 90 days after the application is withdrawn.

CHAPTER 14

Fair Housing Act

Subpart C

Discrimination in Residential Real Estate-Related Transactions

A civil rights law, the Fair Housing Act prohibits discrimination in the sale, rental or advertising of a residential property on the basis of race, color, religion, handicap, sex, familial status or national origin. Any person who is in the business of selling, brokering, appraising, or lending money on real property must comply with the Fair Housing Act.[118]

In cases involving discrimination in mortgage loans or home improvement loans, the Justice Department may file suit under both the Fair Housing Act and the Equal Credit Opportunity Act. The Department brings cases where there is evidence of a pattern or practice of discrimination or where a denial of rights to a group of persons raises an issue of general public importance. Where force or threat of force is used to deny or interfere with fair housing rights, the Department of Justice may institute criminal proceedings.

The Fair Housing Act also provides procedures for handling individual complaints of discrimination. Individuals who believe that they have been victims of an illegal housing practice, may file a complaint with the Department of Housing and Urban Development (HUD) or file their own lawsuit in federal or state court. The Department of Justice brings suits on behalf of individuals based on referrals from HUD.[119]

Subject matter in this chapter includes key sections of Subpart C of the Fair Housing Act, Part 100, and Subpart G, Discriminatory Effect.

§ 100.110

Discriminatory Practices in Residential Real Estate-related Transactions

a) This subpart provides the Department's interpretation of the conduct that is unlawful housing discrimination under section 805 of the Fair Housing Act.

b) It shall be unlawful for any person or other entity whose business includes engaging in residential real estate-related transactions to discriminate against any person in making available such a transaction, or in the terms or conditions of such a transaction, because of race, color, religion, sex, handicap, familial status, or national origin.

§ 100.115

Residential real estate-related transactions

The term residential real estate-related transactions means:

a) The making or purchasing of loans or providing other financial assistance—

1) For purchasing, constructing, improving, repairing or maintaining a dwelling; or

2) Secured by residential real estate; or

b) The selling, brokering or appraising of residential real property.

§ 100.120

Discrimination in the Making of Loans and in the Provision of other Financial Assistance

a) It shall be unlawful for any person or entity whose business includes engaging in residential real estate-related transactions to discriminate against any person in making available loans or other financial assistance for a dwelling, or which is or is to be secured by a dwelling, because of race, color, religion, sex, handicap, familial status, or national origin.

b) Practices prohibited under this section in connection with a residential real estate-related transaction include, but are not limited to:

1) Failing or refusing to provide to any person information regarding the availability of loans or other financial assistance, application requirements, procedures or standards for the review and approval of loans or financial assistance or providing information which is inaccurate or different from that provided to others, because of race, color, religion, sex, handicap, familial status, or national origin.

2) Providing, failing to provide, or discouraging the receipt of loans or other financial assistance in a manner that discriminates in their denial rate or otherwise discriminates in their availability because of race, color, religion, sex, handicap, familial status, or national origin.

3) Conditioning the availability of a loan or other financial assistance on a person's response to harassment because of race, color, religion, sex, handicap, familial status, or national origin.

4) Subjecting a person to harassment because of race, color, religion, sex, handicap, familial status, or national origin that affects the availability of a loan or other financial assistance.

§ 100.125

Discrimination in the Purchasing of Loans

a) It shall be unlawful for any person or entity engaged in the purchasing of loans or other debts or securities which support the purchase, construction, improvement, repair or maintenance of a dwelling, or which are secured by residential real estate, to refuse to purchase such loans, debts, or securities, or to impose different terms or conditions for such purchases, because of race, color, religion, sex, handicap, familial status, or national origin.

b) Unlawful conduct under this section includes, but is not limited to:

1. Purchasing loans or other debts or securities which relate to, or which are secured by dwellings in certain communities or neighborhoods but not in others because of the race, color, religion, sex, handicap, familial status, or national origin of persons in such neighborhoods or communities.

2. Pooling or packaging loans or other debts or securities which relate to, or which are secured by, dwellings differently because of race, color, religion, sex, handicap, familial status, or national origin.

3. Imposing or using different terms or conditions on the marketing or sale of securities issued on the basis of loans or other debts or securities which relate to, or which are secured by, dwellings because of race, color, religion, sex, handicap, familial status, or national origin.

a) This section does not prevent consideration, in the purchasing of loans, of factors justified by business necessity, including requirements of Federal law, relating to a transaction's financial security or to protection against default or reduction of the value of the security. Thus, this provision would not preclude considerations employed in normal and prudent transactions, provided that no such factor may in any way relate to race, color, religion, sex, handicap, familial status or national origin.

Discrimination in the Terms and Conditions for Making Available Loans or other Financial Assistance

a) It shall be unlawful for any person or entity engaged in the making of loans or in the provision of other financial assistance relating to the purchase, construction, improvement, repair or maintenance of dwellings or which are secured by residential real estate to impose different terms or conditions for the availability of such loans or other financial assistance because of race, color, religion, sex, handicap, familial status, or national origin.

b) Unlawful conduct under this section includes, but is not limited to:

1) Using different policies, practices or procedures in evaluating or in determining creditworthiness of any person in connection with the provision of any loan or other financial assistance for a dwelling or for any loan or other financial assistance which is secured by residential real estate because of race, color, religion, sex, handicap, familial status, or national origin.

2) Determining the type of loan or other financial assistance to be provided with respect to a dwelling, or fixing the amount, interest rate, cost, duration or other terms or conditions for a loan or other financial assistance for a dwelling or which is secured by residential real estate, because of race, color, religion, sex, handicap, familial status, or national origin.

3) Servicing of loans or other financial assistance with respect to dwellings in a manner that discriminates, or servicing of loans or other financial assistance which are secured by residential real estate in a manner that discriminates, or providing such loans or financial assistance with other terms or conditions that discriminate, because of race, color, religion, sex, handicap, familial status, or national origin.

4) Conditioning an aspect of a loan or other financial assistance to be provided with respect to a dwelling, or the terms or conditions thereof, on a person's response to harassment because of race, color, religion, sex, handicap, familial status, or national origin.

5) Subjecting a person to harassment because of race, color, religion, sex, handicap, familial status, or national origin that has the effect of imposing different terms or conditions for the availability of such loans or other financial assistance.

§ 100.135

Unlawful Practices in the Selling, Brokering, or Appraising of Residential Real Property

a) It shall be unlawful for any person or other entity whose business includes engaging in the selling, brokering or appraising of residential real property to discriminate against any person in making available such services, or in the performance of such services, because of race, color, religion, sex, handicap, familial status, or national origin.

b) For the purposes of this section, the term appraisal means an estimate or opinion of the value of a specified residential real property made in a business context in connection with the sale, rental, financing or refinancing of a dwelling or in connection with any activity that otherwise affects the availability of a residential real estate-related transaction, whether the appraisal is oral or written, or transmitted formally or informally. The appraisal includes all written comments and other documents submitted as support for the estimate or opinion of value.

c) Nothing in this section prohibits a person engaged in the business of making or furnishing appraisals of residential real property from taking into consideration factors other than race, color, religion, sex, handicap, familial status, or national origin.

d) Practices which are unlawful under this section include, but are not limited to:

1) Using an appraisal of residential real property in connection with the sale, rental, or financing of any dwelling where the person knows or reasonably should know that the appraisal improperly takes into consideration race, color, religion, sex, handicap, familial status, or national origin.

2) Conditioning the terms of an appraisal of residential real property in connection with the sale, rental, or financing of a dwelling on a person's response to harassment because of race, color, religion, sex, handicap, familial status, or national origin.

Subpart G
Discriminatory Effect

Discriminatory Effect Prohibited

Liability may be established under the Fair Housing Act based on a practice's discriminatory effect, as defined in paragraph (a) of this section, even if the practice was not motivated by a discriminatory intent. The practice may still be lawful if supported by a legally sufficient justification, as defined in paragraph (b) of this section. The burdens of proof for establishing a violation under this subpart are set forth in paragraph (c) of this section.

A. Discriminatory effect. A practice has a discriminatory effect where it actually or predictably results in a disparate impact on a group of persons or creates, increases, reinforces, or perpetuates segregated housing patterns because of race, color, religion, sex, handicap, familial status, or national origin.

B. Legally sufficient justification.

1. A legally sufficient justification exists where the challenged practice:

    i.   Is necessary to achieve one or more substantial, legitimate, nondiscriminatory interests of the respondent, with respect to claims brought under 42 U.S.C. 3612, or defendant, with respect to claims brought under 42 U.S.C. 3613 or 3614; and

    ii. Those interests could not be served by another practice that has a less discriminatory effect.

2. A legally sufficient justification must be supported by evidence and may not be hypothetical or speculative. The burdens of proof for establishing each of the two elements of a legally sufficient justification are set forth in paragraphs (c)(2) and (3) of this section.

149

C. Burdens of proof in discriminatory effects cases.

1) The charging party, with respect to a claim brought under 42 U.S.C. 3612, or the plaintiff, with respect to a claim brought under 42 U.S.C. 3613 or 3614, has the burden of proving that a challenged practice caused or predictably will cause a discriminatory effect.

2) Once the charging party or plaintiff satisfies the burden of proof set forth in paragraph (c)(1) of this section, the respondent or defendant has the burden of proving that the challenged practice is necessary to achieve one or more substantial, legitimate, nondiscriminatory interests of the respondent or defendant.

3) If the respondent or defendant satisfies the burden of proof set forth in paragraph (c)(2) of this section, the charging party or plaintiff may still prevail upon proving that the substantial, legitimate, nondiscriminatory interests supporting the challenged practice could be served by another practice that has a less discriminatory effect.

D. Relationship to discriminatory intent. A demonstration that a practice is supported by a legally sufficient justification, as defined in paragraph (b) of this section, may not be used as a defense against a claim of intentional discrimination.

About the Author

Anna DeSimone

A nationally respected expert in fair and responsible mortgage lending, Anna has authored more than 40 compliance handbooks for industry professionals published by AllRegs, Ellie Mae, Freddie Mac, the Federal Reserve Bank of Boston, and numerous industry trade groups.

She has written a dozen publications for the Mortgage Bankers Association of America, including the *Handbook of Fair Lending*, and *the Fair Lending Resource Guide*, commissioned by President Clinton under a White House Executive Order to help curb lending discrimination.

Anna was founder and CEO of Bankers Advisory, a Massachusetts-based quality control and compliance audit services firm, now Clifton Larson Allen Mortgage Advisory Services. She provides fair lending consulting services and policy development to financial institutions.

www.housingresearchpress.com

Books by Anna DeSimone
www.annadesimone.net

Live in a Home that Pays You Back
Living Now, Silver Medal in Nature Conservation
Pinnacle Book Achievement Award

Welcome to the Agrihood
Pinnacle Book Achievement Award
Living Now Book Award

Housing Finance 2020
Axiom Book Award
Silver Medalist in Personal Finance, Retirement Planning and Investing

Hipoteca 2020
(Spanish Edition)

Notes

[1] *State of the Nation's Housing Report 2023*, Joint Center for Housing Studies of Harvard University.

[2] *Snapshot of Race and Homebuying in America,* Statista, February 29, 2024.

[3] Ibid.

[4] *Black Wealth is Increasing, but so is the Wealth Gap,* Andre M. Perry, Hannah Stephens, and Manann Donoghoe, Brookings Institute, January 9, 2024.

[5] *State of the Nation's Housing Report 2023*, Joint Center for Housing Studies of Harvard University.

[6] Ibid.

[7] U.S. Department of the Treasury, Office of Economic Policy, Racial Differences in Economic Security: Housing, November 4, 2022.

[8] *2020 Census Illuminates Racial and Ethnic Composition of the Country*, U.S. Census Bureau, August 12, 2021.

[9] HUD Ownership and Vacancy Report, Q3 2021.

[10] *2020 Census Illuminates Racial and Ethnic Composition of the Country*, U.S. Census Bureau, August 12, 2021.

[11] HUD Ownership and Vacancy Report, Q3 2021.

[12] *New Report on the Nation's Foreign-Born Population*, U.S. Census Bureau,   April 9, 2024.

[13] Ibid.

[14] *2020 Census Illuminates Racial and Ethnic Composition of the Country*, U.S. Census Bureau, August 12, 2021.

[15] *State of the Nation's Housing Report 2023,* Joint Center for Housing Studies of Harvard University.

[16] Justice Department and CFPB Joint Statement on Fair Lending and Credit Opportunities for Non-citizen Borrowers, October 13, 2023.

[17] Federal Reserve Report on Economic Well-Being, May 2023.

[18] *Survey of Household Economics and Decisionmaking,* October 2021-November 2022, Federal Reserve Board, May 2023.

[19] *State of the Nation's Housing Report 2023*, Joint Center for Housing Studies of Harvard University.

[20] U.S. Census Bureau, American Community Survey, 2021.

[21] *State of the Nation's Housing Report 2023*, Joint Center for Housing Studies of Harvard University.

[22] *2024 Snapshot of Race and Homebuying in America,* National Association of Realtors.

[23] *Indoor Air Quality in Multifamily Housing,* Environmental Pro-tection Agency.

[24] *National and State Cost Savings Associated With Prohibiting Smoking in Subsidized and Public Housing in the United States,* Cen-ters for Disease Control and Prevention (CDC), King BA, Peck RM, Babb SD, Prev Chronic Dis 014;11:140222

[25] *Capturing the Multiple Benefits of Energy Efficiency,* International Energy Agency, March 2019.

[26] *Credits and Deductions under the Inflation Reduction Act of 2022,* Internal Revenue Service.

[27] Fannie Mae *HomeStyle Energy*; Freddie Mac *GreenChoice.*

[28] NC Clean Energy Technology Center.

[29] *State of the Nation's Housing Report 2023*, Joint Center for Housing Studies, Harvard University, March 2024.

[30] Fannie Mae, *Disaster Help for Homeowners*.

[31] St. Louis Federal Reserve Bank, September 2023.

[32] Federal Housing Finance Agency, House Price Index.

[33] Ibid.

[34] FHFA HPI Quarterly Report, February 27, 2024.

[35] *Why House Prices Surged as The COVID-19 Pandemic Took Hold,* John V. Duca and Anthony Murphy, Federal Reserve Bank of Dallas, December 28, 2021

[36] NAREB Building Black Wealth Tour.

[37] HUD Announces Pivotal Partnership with NAREB, HUD Exchange, August 2, 2023.

[38] NAREB *State of Black Housing in America, 2023 Report.*

[39] The Hispanic Wealth Project.

[40] *2023 State of Hispanic Housing Report,* National Association of Hispanic Real Estate Professionals.

[41] *HMDA Data Points 2022,* Consumer Financial Protection Bureau.

[42] FFIEC/CFPB, HMDA data, 2021.

[43] U.S. Census Bureau, 2021 American Community Survey, 5-year Estimates.

[44] Consumer Financial Protection Bureau, HMDA Quarterly Graphs.

[45] Consumer Financial Protection Bureau, HMDA Data Points 2020-2022

[46] Ibid.

[47] *Lender-Reported Reasons for Mortgage Denials Don't Explain Racial Disparities,* Federal Reserve Bank of Minneapolis, Ben Horowitz, Libby Starling, and Kim-Eng Ky, January 18, 2024.

[48] Ibid.

[49] Ibid.

[50] Equal Credit Opportunity Act (ECOA)

[51] Ibid.

[52] Federal Trade Commission, Credit Score Disclosure. [53] CFPB Circular 2022-03

[54] *An AI Fair Lending Policy Agenda,* Brookings Institute, 12/2/2021

[55] Office of Public Affairs, U.S. Department of Justice, 3/5/24.

[56] *2023 State of Housing in Black America*, James H. Carr and Michela Zonta, commissioned by the National Association of Real Estate Brokers, November 12, 2023.

[57] *What Do Borrowers Do When a Mortgage Application Is Denied*, Freddie Mac Research Brief, August 19 2022.

[58] *March 2024 Consumer Response Annual Report,* CFPB.

[59] *Justice Department Announces New Initiative to Combat Redlining*, DOJ Press Release, October 22, 2021.

[60] *Federal Reserve History--Redlining,* Federal Reserve Bank of St. Louis, June 2, 2023.

[61] Ibid.

[62] *NCRC Study: More Chronic Disease, Shorter Lifespans And Greater Risk Factors For COVID-19 In Neighborhoods That Were Redlined 80 Years Ago*, National Coalition for Community Reinvestment, September 10, 2020

[63] *Justice Department Announces New Initiative to Combat Redlining*, DOJ Press Release, October 22, 2021.

[64] *Which Lenders are More Likely to Reach Out to Underserved Consumers, Banks vs. Fintechs vs. Other Nonbanks*, Federal Reserve Bank of New York, 9/29/2022

[65] Director Chopra's Prepared Remarks at Justice Department Interagency Event in Newark, New Jersey to Highlight Efforts to Combat Modern-Day Redlining, CFPB Newsroom, April 19, 2023

[66] *Justice Department and Consumer Financial Protection Bureau Sue Texas-Based Developer and Lender Colony Ridge for Bait-and-Switch Land Sales and Predatory Financing*, DOJ Press Release December 20, 2023

[67] Equal Credit Opportunity Act, Title 12, Chapter II, Subchapter A, CFR.

[68] U.S. Department of Housing and Urban Development, *Discriminatory Effects Standard, March 23, 2023.*

[69] Foothold Technology, Human Services Software Program Data.

[70] Federal Housing Finance Agency, Appraisal Gap Dashboard.

[71] Financial Housing Finance Agency, Appraisal Gap Calculation.

[72] FHFA, UAD Aggregate Statistics, State and County Dashboard.

[73] U.S. Department of Justice, Press Release 6/13/2023.

[74] *Home Appraised with a Black Owner: $472,000, with a White Owner: $750,000*, New York Times, Deborah Kamin, 6/1/23.

[75] *Reducing Valuation Bias by Addressing Appraiser and Property Valuation*, FHFA Commentary, 12/14/2021

[76] *Underappraisal Disparities and Time Adjustments*, FHFA Blog, 1/16/24

[77] *Unacceptable Appraisal Practices*, Freddie Mac, January 30, 2024

[78] FDIC Press Release, 6/21/2023.

[79] *Freddie Mac, Fannie Mae, and HUD issue policy and procedure requirements for appraisal ROVs,* Freddie Mac Guide Bulletin 2024-6, May 1, 2024.

[80] *Mortgage borrowers can challenge inaccurate appraisals through the reconsideration of value process,* CFPB Blog, October 6, 2022.

[81] Interagency Task Force on Property Appraisal and Valuation Equity (PAVE).

[82] Consumer Financial Protection Bureau.

[83] *Biden-Harris Administration Tackles Racial and Ethnic Bias in Home Valuations,* PAVE Critical Progress, March 23, 2023.

[84] *Statement on Examination Principles Related to Valuation Discrimination and Bias in Residential Lending,* Federal Financial Institutions Examination Council February 12, 2024.

[85] *HUD Announces Pivotal Partnership with NAREB,* HUD Exchange, August 2, 2023.

[86] Uniform Standards of Professional Appraisal Practice (USPAP).

[87] *Share of Non-Qualified Mortgages Increases in 2022,* Archana Pradhan, Principal, Economist, Office of the Chief Economist, Core Logic, June 1. 2022.

[88] Ibid.

[89] *Using Special Purpose Credit Programs to Serve Unmet Needs,* Tim Lambert, CFPB blog, July 19, 2022.

[90] *Three Halal Mortgage Options for Muslims in the U.S.,* Blog, Musaffa Academy.

[91] 2021 National Survey of Unbanked and Underbanked Households, FDIC.

[92] FFIEC, February 2021 BSA/AML Examination Manual.

[93] *More than 45 Million Americans are Either Credit Unserved or Underserved,* TransUnion, April 7, 2022.

[94] *Financial Inclusion And Access To Credit,* Oliverwyman, 2022.

[95] *Downpayment Toward Equity Act of 2024*, H.R. 4231, U.S. Congress.

[96] *Summary of First Generation Down Payment Fund*, National Council of State Housing Agencies, December 9, 2021.

[97]HUD Program Offices, Single Family, Housing Counseling.

[98] Ibid.

[99] *Housing Counseling Works 2023 Update*, Katina E. Norwood and Marina L. Myhre, HUD, January 23, 2024.

[100] Let's Make Home the Goal, HUD.

[101] Consumer Financial Protection Bureau, Consumer Resources

[102]Fannie Mae, HomeView.

[103] Fannie Mae, Talk to a Counselor.

[104] Freddie Mac, CreditSmart Homebuyer U.

[105] Freddie Mac, Borrower Help Center.

[106] Fannie Mae, HomeReady First.

[107] Ibid.

[108] Homeowners Protection Act, Private Mortgage Insurance Cancelation.

[109] Wall Street Reform and Consumer Protection Act (Dodd-Frank).

[110] Consumer Financial Protection Bureau, QM/ATR Rule.

[111] Ibid.

[112] Ibid.

[113] Ibid.

[114] Ibid.

[115] Equal Credit Opportunity Act, Title 12, Chapter II, Subchapter A, Code of Federal Regulations, National Archives, February 24, 2024.

[116] U.S. Department of Justice, Civil Rights Division, The Equal Credit Opportunity Act, January 25, 2024.

[117] Ibid.

[118] Fair Housing Act, Title 24, Subpart C, Discrimination in Residential Real Estate- Related Transactions, February 12, 2024.

[119] U.S. Department of Justice, Civil Rights Division, The Fair Housing Act.

www.ingramcontent.com/pod-product-compliance
Lightning Source LLC
Chambersburg PA
CBHW061021220326
41597CB00016BB/2064